A MAN OF MIRACLES

BY: Heather Parsons

ISBN#1-891280-58-9

Publisher:
CMJ Marian Publishers
and Distributors
Post Office Box 661
Oak Lawn, Illinois 60453
Tel: 708-636-2995 / Fax: 708-636-2855
Toll Free: 1-888-636-6799
http://www.cmjbooks.com
jwby@aol.com

Manufactured in the United States of America

Graphic Design: Pete Massari

Formerly under title: Man of Miracles
Copyrighted 1994 Heather Parsons and published by the
Guernsey Press Company

Photo on cover provided with permission to copy by:
Sylvester Markowski
South Milwaukee, Wisconsin
2005

To Father Peter, with my love and prayers always... to all those who shared the remarkable stories of their healings... and to my family.

CONTENTS

Foreword

I first met Fr Peter Rookey in 1988 when he visited Radio Telefis Eireann where I work, to take part in a television programme. His kindness, concern and humour, his obvious deep faith and his love for all those he met made a deep impression on me.

I had heard about him of course, the 'famous healing priest' from Chicago who apparently performed miracles. Many years as a journalist had taught me to be cautious about such claims, but curious, I attended one of Fr Peter's Healing Masses.

What I experienced there has never left me. Although with a deep faith in God, I had never realised how powerfully He is still working in the world today, performing miracles that I had thought restricted to biblical days, healing people in body and spirit and undoubtedly, I admitted to myself, working with love through this holy and humble man.

It was 1989 when I first visited Fr Peter in Chicago and I have been privileged to meet with him on many occasions ever since, in many different places.

Two years ago I felt that I was being asked to write a book about his ministry, not for the glory of Fr Peter who is the last person to wish for such, but for the honour and glory of God whose power we limit so severely in this 'rational' world of ours. I was touched when Fr Peter — who has had many such requests from authors and journalists all over the world, but who up to then not given his approval to anybody — gave me his blessing to go ahead.

The following is the book that emerged, a story of the man and his ministry, but especially of the powerful, loving and healing presence of Jesus in the world today.

I dedicate it to Fr Peter with love, and in appeal to the Holy Spirit to continue to use him as an instrument of God's healing in this world for many years to come.

HEATHER PARSONS April 1994.

The Miracle Prayer

Lord Jesus, I come before you, just as I am. I am sorry for my sins, I repent of my sins, please forgive me. In your name I forgive all others for what they have done against me. I renounce satan, the evil spirits and all their works. I give you my entire self, Lord Jesus, now and forever. I invite you into my life Jesus, I accept you as my Lord, God and Saviour. Heal me, change me, strengthen me in body, soul and spirit.
Come Lord Jesus, cover me with your precious blood, and fill me with your Holy Spirit. I love you Lord Jesus. I praise you Jesus. I thank you Jesus. I shall follow you every day of my life.
Amen.

Mary my mother, Queen of Peace, all the Angels and Saints please help me. Amen.

Imprimatur † Francisco Maris Aguilera Gonzalez,
Auxiliary Bishop of Mexico, September 8, 1992

Say this Prayer faithfully, no matter how you feel, when you come to the point where you sincerly mean each word, with all your heart, something good spiritually will happen to you. You will experience Jesus, and HE will change your whole life in a very special way. You will see.

Chapter One

OUT OF THE DARKNESS

It was the darkness more than the pain that frightened him.

All round him he heard the voices, some he knew, some strange.

His mother was there. The feel of her hand on his forehead, holding his hand, consoled him.

Putting a hand to his face he felt the bandages that wound round his head, across his eyes.

Everything had changed. The world was different, strange, now that he could no longer see what went on around him.

They had explained to him that his eyes had been damaged. He heard the word 'destroyed' and despite the pain couldn't help wondering what his eyes, his face looked like. Did he look frightening, like some sort of monster? Would people run away from him on the street? Would the other kids be afraid to come near him?

And would this darkness ever go?

He remembered, once, closing his eyes and pretending to be blind. It was a scary feeling. He kept bumping into things and finally decided to give it up when he bumped into the side of a door and left an egg-shaped swelling on his forehead.

Scary, because he felt completely disorientated not being able to see what was around him, but exciting too because he knew that any moment he could, if he wished, open his eyes and the world would be normal again.

This was different. They had changed the bandages on his eyes several times and each time he had seen nothing, not even a faint glimpse of light.

The last thing he could remember seeing was the firecracker, just before it exploded in his face.

It had been an ordinary sort of day up to that.The fourth of July celebrations were over and the city of Superior, Wisconsin had played itself out. Everybody seemed to be in a lazy mood, he thought, as he and his younger brother Bernard wandered down a street near their home.

Superior could be a cold city, based as it was on the western most end of Lake Superior. Today though was hot, the sun beating down on Peter's eight year old shoulders as he and Bernard kicked an empty can they found, before pitching it into a nearby garbage drum, just like they'd seen their older brothers pitching at baseball games.

A couple of minutes later they'd seen it. A huge fire cracker lying in the gutter. He and Bernard had dashed up to it, both wanting to claim ownership. From the look of it somebody had tried to light it, but when it had failed to go off they'd thrown it away.

What a find!

They brought it home and out into the back yard. It was bound to go miles up into the sky and explode with a great noise and plenty of coloured flames, Peter told Bernard as he lit the damaged fuse.

Disappointingly, it wouldn't go off. Maybe it needed a little help, Peter said, holding it up to see exactly where the problem might be, then blowing as hard as he could to ignite the smouldering fuse.

All he remembered after that was a huge explosion, as the fire cracker blew up right into his face, the searing pain wiping out the next few days.

He was blind, his mother explained to him gently. The doctors had done everything they could, but at the end of the day there wasn't a lot they could do except change the bandages regularly to prevent infection.

He could hear Dr Barnsdahl explaining to his mother, as he expertly changed the dressings, that the damage was too great. The boy would never see again.

And his mother's voice, clear and strong as she took him home, 'We'll see about that. From today we'll say the Rosary especially for your healing'.

"That was where it all began," says Fr Peter Rookey, holding up his hands in the air as an expression of the inevitability of it all, almost seventy years later, sight restored and a lifetime of service to God and witness to the healing power of Christ behind him.

"I suppose you could say it was the first miracle I witnessed and one I couldn't deny because it happened to me.

"I was blind for a long time. It seemed like an eternity to me, because I was so young and it made life so different, but in real terms it was about a year and a half.

"My healing was gradual and was all due to faith and prayer."

His mother was the driving force, he recalls.

Johanna McGarry, one of twenty children all born in the United States, was brought up with a strong sense of Irish identity and Catholic values. Her father, from County

Limerick, Ireland and her mother, also Irish (whose maiden name was Byron) instilled a deep belief in the power of God into the young Johanna as she grew up.

She met Anthony Daniel Routhier (later changed to Rookey because so many mis-spelled and mispronounced the name) soon after she began teaching. Routhier, born in Alexandria in the province of Ontario, Canada to an Irish mother and French father (who had met when they both stepped onto American soil from emigrant ships) had left Canada in search of better work opportunities. His search led him, eventually, to the town of Stillwater, Minnesota, where he found work as a logger.

One night, at a social, he met the young school-teacher who was to become his wife. In many ways they couldn't have been more different, Johanna so strong-minded, independent and full of confidence, Anthony so quiet, mild-mannered but with an in-built determination to find his way in the world.

"But they shared something very important," Fr Peter recalls, his eyes fixed outwardly on the wall opposite where he is sitting, but inwardly on the two people who hold a special place in his heart.

"They were both full of fun and love, with a wonderful sense of humour."

They had married and settled in Superior, Wisconsin where Anthony Rookey went into the dray business, starting with a wagon and horses and hauling for Standard Oil.

Those were good days, Fr Peter recalls with a smile.

"If we were good boys, we were allowed to hold the horses' reins."

In time, the horses gave way to lorries and trucks and Anthony Rookey branched out into the Rookey Transfer Company with the franchise for United Van Lines.

The uniquely Irish tradition of large families carried down to Fr Peter's generation. Eighteen of his mother's family had survived childhood; his father had been one of eleven and Johanna and Anthony themselves had thirteen children, Peter coming ninth in line.

Their Catholic faith was very much part of the family life. Sunday and weekday Mass, devotions, the evening Rosary.

"My mother was a very devout person," Fr Peter says.

"And very beautiful. I remember one of the Servite priests in our area was helping to give a Mission at the Cathedral in Superior and he told my mother he was going to bring her up on the pulpit when he spoke about abortion and birth control, as an example to the congregation.

"There was a lot of talk those days that having large families was unhealthy, and that it wore out women, turning them into old hags. But my mother was so beautiful and full of energy and so happy that she belied the whole thing. Besides bringing up a large family, she ran my father's office. She was what I suppose you might describe as a loving disciplinarian, well able to balance everything in her busy life."

Over the next months Johanna McGarry Rookey, in total confidence, led her family in prayer for Peter's healing. The family Rosary was dedicated each night for the return of his eyesight, a healing that she was quite sure would come about if it was at all in God's plans. The devotions were increased and when May came round, Johanna set up a special May altar in the attic of the large three-story house that was home to her family and sought increased intercession of the Virgin Mary, to whom she had a deep devotion.

"My mother's faith was such that I never doubted her belief that if it was God's wish my sight would return.

"I asked the Lord to heal me and I promised Him that if he gave me back my sight I would become a priest. In my mind the two things were intertwined. Obviously I couldn't become a priest if I was blind.

"And gradually, despite the doctor's warnings that we were hoping in vain, my sight began to return until finally it was restored.

"Obviously, it was a miracle. There was no other explanation."

It was also the first step in faith towards a life devoted to Jesus and Mary.

At thirteen years of age, Peter Rookey left the Sacred Heart Grammar School in Superior for the Servite seminary of Mater Dolorosa at Hillside in Chicago, Illinois, some five hundred miles from his home and family.

The years in the seminary he recalls with a mixture of happiness and humour. His first novice master was a Fr Joseph Srill, to be succeeded three years later by Irishman Fr John Keane, a strict and holy man who, as it turned out, was to become Fr Peter's Superior when among seven priests they travelled to Benburb, County Tyrone to found the Servite order in Ireland.

"When we served Mass, Fr Keane expected us servers to be perfect. He demanded perfection in everything and used to quote Michelangelo: 'Perfection is made up of trifles, but perfection is no trifle'."

The irrepressible humour that Fr Peter inherited from his parents breaks out as he recalls some of the escapades he and his fellow seminarians got up to. Laughingly, he tells of one particular misdemeanour that occurred just after the exams and before the summer vacation, when students were allowed home to spend time with their families.

"We were on the top floor of the seminary," he laughs, shaking his head at the memory.

"The student quarters and our dormitory looked out over the main street, Hillside Avenue. We had made up a scarecrow from various bits and pieces so that it looked like a real man. We waited until people were going by on the sidewalk, then just as they got near the building we screamed and shouted to attract their attention, then heaved the scarecrow out of the window.

"Needless to say, the Prior did not find this at all funny."

The love and care for others that is so evident to anybody who comes in contact with Fr Peter Rookey, extends beyond death to the souls of those who might need his prayers.

Close to the Servite seminary was a cemetery, now the largest in the arch-diocese of Chicago, where most of the gangsters who once ruled Chicago life lie buried.

"We used to walk through this cemetery, Our Lady Queen of Heaven as it is called, and pray for the gangsters who were buried there. We saw many a gangster procession over those years. They sent the boys off in grand style you know, with a bus for the band and an open Cadillac or two filled with orchids, some of them from the very gang that had bumped off the mobster who was being buried.

"Al Capone was buried there and sometimes I'd go by and pray at his grave, or at the graves of Diamond Joe Brady, the famous Irish gangster, or Legs Diamond."

There were times, he admits, when he felt like leaving the seminary and returning to his large, noisy and fun-loving family for whom he was very homesick during those early years. But thank God, as he now says himself, he overcame that with the help of his fellow students and the support and encouragement of the priests who served in the seminary.

His ordination on May 17th 1941 was followed by two and a half years in Milwaukee, Wisconsin where he was assistant to the novice master at the Servite novitiate and college; four years in Portland, Oregon, the beautiful national Servite shrine to Our Sorrowful Mother where he gained a wealth of experience in parish work; then one year teaching in the Servite seminary in Hillside, Chicago before leaving for Ireland in August 1948 to help Fr John Mary Keane found the new Servite order in Benburb.

Strangely, it was in Ireland, the land of his ancestors, that Fr Peter Mary Rookey first came to realise that Jesus, in all His power and glory, had mapped out a very special role for him as an instrument of His love and healing power in the lives of thousands whose pain and suffering, both physical and spiritual, He wished to relieve.

Chapter Two

"I COULD SEE!"

Patrick Magee eased the car through the crowds and parked as close as possible to the new Servite Priory in Benburb.

The day was clear but cold as he and his wife May made their way along with many others, some of whom had come in the buses parked outside, to where the young Servite priest was blessing the sick.

They'd heard all about him. The whole province of Ulster seemed to be talking about him. He performed miracles, people said. Accounts flew around of the many healings that were being attributed to his prayers.

At first, only a trickle of people had come to the new priory that first year, 1948, seeking blessing and consolation in their troubles and illnesses. But as word spread that miracles were happening when the young American priest prayed, people came in their hundreds so that soon, it was no longer possible to cope with them all in the small chapel and the 'healing' services had to be held out of doors.

Patrick Magee clutched his daughter protectively in his arms, as the baby's sightless eyes seemed to gaze at the scene in front of them.

At eight months old, Patricia was the centre of her parents' love and devotion. Looking at their beautiful little daughter, Patrick and May's hearts broke for her.

Never would she be able to live a normal life. Never would she see the dawn break or the sun set, or gasp in wonder at the bees as they gathered honey from brightly coloured flowers. Against the brightness of her personality, the darkness of her world seemed impossible to accept.

Patrick stood beside May as they patiently waited their turn.

Thank God he had made an appointment. Never had he seen so many people. There must be a two mile tailback of traffic Patrick thought, but he and May had been led right up to the front.

The crowds thronged round the black-robed figure, threatening to crush him, but the young priest with his warm smile and gentle touch never lost patience, moving from one person to another, holding his hands over their heads, blessing them with a crucifix he held in the palm of his right hand, a cross that held the relic, Patrick later learned, of the Servite Saint Philip Benizi.

It was some time before Fr Rookey came to where Patrick and May were standing, still holding Patricia.

Fleeting thoughts had been going through Patrick's mind as he waited. Maybe they were crazy, hoping that a miracle could happen for them. If he had told Patricia's doctors they would certainly have thought him crazy to even contemplate such a happening.

Nothing could be done for Patricia, they had told her parents firmly, if sadly. She had been born with detached retina in both eyes. There was no operation they could perform that would give her sight.

And yet, as the priest stopped in front of them, Patrick Magee felt a strange sensation that he was doing the right thing.

Fr Rookey laid his hands on the little girl's head, then touched her eyes, blessing her with the cross and praying over her before finally telling them to pray 'Our Lady and St Philip Benizi, pray for us' several times each day and always during the Rosary.

"Your child will see," he said.

And then he was gone, moving on to the next person.

It was quiet in the car as they returned home to Belfast.

Nothing had happened. Patricia's sight had not been restored and yet, the feeling of peace they had experienced in Benburb stayed with them.

Patrick and May began to pray the Rosary, while in the back Patricia bounced up and down on her grandmother's knee. As the child reached up to pull at the window-blind, her grandmother caught her breath. It couldn't be true, she thought, momentarily speechless.

But yes... "Suddenly, I could see," Patricia says today.

"The sight that the doctors said I would never have, was given to me as a gift from God through the prayers of this priest.

"My parents and grandmother were so excited. They couldn't believe it at first."

Patricia herself has no memories of that great moment in her life when, suddenly and unexpectedly, her world turned from dark to light.

Her next meeting with Fr Peter Rookey, in the community centre beside St Agnes Parish Church in Belfast well over thirty years later, was an emotional one for both of them.

Fr Peter was in Belfast for a healing service when a neighbour visited Patricia's home. Mentioning casually that crowds of people had been pouring into St Agnes' church hall where a Father Rookey was holding a service, she was taken aback when Patricia's mother suddenly grabbed her coat and dashed out the door.

Running down the road, into the hall and straight up to the priest, May stopped to look at him closely then burst into tears. "I thought you were dead," she wept, before falling into Father Peter's arms as she told him the story.

The next evening Patricia and her mother attended the healing service. When Father Peter asked whether there was anybody in the congregation who would like to share what Christ had done in their lives, Patricia moved up to the microphone and in front of over one thousand people told her story.

Was it a miracle, a local reporter later asked her?

"All I know," she replied quietly, "was that I was blind, and now I can see."

In over fifty years in the priesthood, Fr Peter Rookey has travelled all over the world, from the United States to South America, Britain, Europe and as far away as the Philippines. The five years he spent in Northern Ireland drew him deeply into the healing ministry, not through any intention of his own, but as the firstly rather surprised, humbled but willing instrument of the Saviour who showed so clearly that He intended to use the young priest as the channel of His healing for so many.

As the years passed, the crowds continued to come to Benburb. When the healed came back to tell their stories and thank the young Servite, he told them the healings could not be laid to his account, but that all glory and honour must be given to the God he represented and to the saints, particularly St Peregrine — the Servite who had a miraculous personal cure from cancer as a young man, in much the same way that Peter Rookey had his own miraculous healing from blindness in his youth — and St

Philip Benizi who was a doctor and who seemed to be particularly powerful with children. The crucifix Fr Peter used to bless the sick contained the relics of these and other Servite saints.

Fr Rookey shakes his head at the suggestion that God has favoured Him.

"The Lord told us to go out to the towns and villages and heal the sick, tell them the kingdom of heaven is at hand," he says, "and so I feel that all priests are called to a greater or lesser degree to take part in the healing ministry of Christ."

Yet, not all priests who pray with people and call on God's power are used as instruments of His healing, I remind him.

Fr Peter considers the remark, passing the large black beads of the Seven Dolours rosary through his hands, head held to one side, a lifetime of genuine humility in the face of his great 'gift' leaving him unable to admit that he has been singled out in any way.

"Well," he says finally. "Perhaps it's the feeling of inadequacy or of fear that acts as a barrier. What if this person is not healed of cancer or blindness or whatever she has... what do I do then? How embarrassing it would be for me — thoughts like that.

"But of course if you stop to realise that it's God who does the healing, that we just pray and it's God who performs the miracles, then we can not claim any merits from the healings and neither can we be held accountable when healings do not occur — it's God's work not ours."

Wherever he goes in the world tremendous crowds flock to him, hoping and praying that the 'healing priest' will work a miracle on their behalf. Many are cured, of everything from cancer to deafness to multiple sclerosis and almost every other illness imaginable. Others go away, bitterly disappointed that they have not been among those to receive the healings so liberally poured out on those around them.

Does the weight of his ministry burden him, faced as he is with the expectations of so many who are ill in body, mind and soul?

"No," he replies, shaking his head as if to emphasise the point.

"I just cast my burdens on the Lord and He sustains me. And I remind myself that I can do nothing. I am just a sinner, a broken vessel, the unworthy instrument of God's healing graces."

The many healing Masses I have attended with Fr Peter go through my mind. In Ireland, the United States, Bosnia-Herzegovina. Times when I have stood or knelt in a church or hall in total awe of the power of God, working so powerfully through the black-robed Servant of Mary. Times when, like so many in the congregations, I have felt the tears pouring down my face as one miraculous happening after another took place in front of my eyes — trained eyes that, after twenty-five years as a journalist are quick to see the false and the fake, and to accept nothing that has not been investigated and proved to my satisfaction.

Observing Fr Peter in his worldwide International Compassion Ministry, I have watched scenes reminiscent of the New Testament stories, when Jesus poured out His love and healing on the crowds who followed Him. Packed churches that could hold perhaps a thousand people comfortably, chosen for their size as being suitable for one of Fr Rookey's healing Masses yet totally inadequate to cope with the thousands that turn up in search of healing, so that the doors must be closed to prevent crushing. People waiting four and five deep outside until those who have been blessed come out, to be replaced by others waiting patiently.

The sick pushing forward to the altar, many in wheelchairs, supported by friends or relatives, children carried in their parents' arms, even some on stretchers, wrapped in blankets, drips held over them.

One picture has never left my mind, from a healing Mass in a packed church in an area of high unemployment in Dublin, Ireland. A young woman was carried in on a stretcher, motionless and wrapped in a blue blanket, the stretcher carried through the packed crowds by six men and brought right up onto the altar steps where Fr Rookey was blessing the sick.

She had been in a coma for two months, he was told. Her family and friends were frantic. All through that time there had been no sign that she was aware of anything around her, no visible sign of life although with the aid of modern medicine her body was being kept alive.

They had taken a chance on bringing her out of the hospital and travelling several miles to the healing Mass, they knew. But they believed that if God wished, He could heal her.

His face full of love and tenderness, Fr Peter laid both hands on the girl's head, anointing her with holy oil, blessing her with the crucifix containing the relics of the seven Servite saints. And as he prayed, eyes closed as he called on the healing power of Jesus and the intercession of Mary and the saints, tears suddenly sprang from the girl's eyes and rolled down her cheeks. Tears that were echoed by everybody who surrounded her.

Was she healed? I never knew. Certainly she did not get up from her stretcher like the man in the Gospel and walk away, but tears are a sign of healing, they say, and perhaps her healing was a gradual one. In the crush that surrounded me I was unable to get out of the church for several minutes. And when I did the stretcher and its bearers were gone.

Why doesn't God heal everybody, instantly, I ask Fr Peter, that incident strongly in my mind?

"I'm afraid that's a question you'll have to put to Him," Fr Peter replies.

"The Spirit of God blows where it will, but in many cases I believe it's a great grace to have a gradual healing rather than an instantaneous one, in the sense that as I pray for my healing I am open to complete healing. I am enriched by my continual prayer and I am becoming holier that way.

"Perhaps the Lord foresees that this is the better way for some people, although on the other hand the instant healing is such a powerful grace that often the person's life turns around.

"Take St Paul for example. In being knocked off his horse he was given a very powerful impulse from the Lord, a complete conversion. But then again I often think of St Monica and her son St Augustine. For thirty to forty years she prayed for this son of hers that she loved so much, but who led such a very bad life. Perhaps if she hadn't had to pray all those years she would just have been a Monica, lost in history. But as it was, she became a saint along with the one for whom she was praying.

"Very often, I have seen in this ministry, that when people are concerned for the healing of others, and pray for that healing, then they too are healed of whatever illness they suffer from."

Chapter Three

A MEETING WITH GOD

'Dear Fr Rookey,

How can we thank you for the many blessings received here from your visit. And more to the point, where to begin? After the healing Mass, the elderly gentleman in the wheelchair that got up and walked out with his wife caused quite a stir in the parish. Two years ago he had a stroke and had not walked since. He is a well known and loved parishioner and his grandson attends our primary school. The morning after the healing service, his grandson (aged almost seven years) stood up in the school assembly and told the whole school: 'Jesus made a miracle in our church last night. My Grandad has not walked for two years and last night, when we all prayed, he got up and walked out... AND that's a miracle.' I understand that the headmaster although a baptised Catholic did not go to Mass any more, but after that witness he asked the staff about the healing Mass and has said he will come back to the Church. Many others also had their faith renewed that evening. Praise God.' (England)

Ruth Allan can vividly remember the day she was told she had cancer. In many ways the news was not unexpected. Her grandmother had died from cancer of the breast and strangely, at the back of her mind had always been the thought that she would suffer the same fate. An idle thought, perhaps, but one that struck her now and then, especially when she prayed for the souls of departed family members.

She had first noticed the tiny lump while showering. Generally, her life being so busy, her morning shower was a rushed affair. This particular day however, a Saturday and one that for some reason or other she had no particular place to go, she allowed herself the luxury of a long soak under the warm water.

She didn't quite believe it when she found the lump. And it felt so small that surely it could mean nothing.

Then the fear hit her — and the recollection of her grandmother's fate.

For several months she allowed that fear to dominate her life, unwilling to go to the doctor in case he told her what she didn't want to hear. And all the time hoping against hope that the lump would disappear.

It didn't. In fact, it grew larger and as time went by Ruth felt less well, less full of energy, at times dragging herself round the place. Finally confiding the fear to her sister, she found the problem taken out of her hands as an urgent appointment was made to visit the family doctor.

The couple of weeks after that passed in a blur. Her family doctor immediately referred her for hospital tests and finally, somebody spoke the words she had been terrified to hear. The lump was malignant. Ruth felt as though a death sentence had been passed on her.

She had already lost valuable time, they told her. An immediate operation was necessary.

She survived that first operation.

"How? I don't know. I was so sure, going into that anaesthetic, that I would never come out of it alive. When

I did I cried for two solid days. A partial removal had been impossible and they'd had to remove my left breast.

"I felt ill, weak, in pain, but most of all scarred — and I don't mean the operation scars. I felt as though a vital part of myself had been taken away. I didn't want my husband and family to come near me. I felt deformed, less than a woman. It took me a long time to come to terms with the effects of the operation.

"Then just when I thought that life couldn't possibly be any worse, I discovered I was wrong. I began a course of chemotherapy. People have different reactions to this treatment, I believe. Mine couldn't have been worse. I was terribly ill after each session. I lost a huge amount of weight and then my hair began to fall out. That was the last straw. I just couldn't face the world. Any time I had to go out, I wore a wig. I didn't even want my family to see me like that, so I wound turbans round my head and used the heaviest make-up possible."

It was summer by now, one of the hottest she could remember in the state of Florida. The intense heat and humidity sapped her strength still further. Her husband and family finally persuaded her to leave her suburban home and go to a beach house on the coast, owned by close friends. Normally, it would have been a heaven-sent break for Ruth, who as Personnel Manager of a large company more often found that her work time strayed far over into what was supposed to be her leisure time.

Feeling ill and weak, it seemed a cruel parody of a vacation.

And yet, she recalls, it was there at the beach house that she came to terms with what was happening to her body. Her family were completely supportive, there when she needed them, but giving her as much space and time alone as she found necessary.

Early morning on the beach, before the heat of the day built up, was her best time. Soon her mornings fell into a pattern as she awoke early and leaving the rest of the household sleeping, walked alone down the deserted sands. Often this would be just after dawn, the remains of the sunrise spreading across the skyline, the beach looking whiter than at any other time during the day, the tips of the waves painted gently white to match the sand they rippled in upon.

It was there, she believes, alone on the beach, that she began to come back to the God of her childhood, long ignored as her busy life took up every waking moment. A small thin figure sitting silently on the dry sand, looking out across the ocean, she thought long and often about life and death, and the life that in her childhood she had been promised came after death.

Home again, stronger and more peaceful, she took to going down to Mass at the local parish church, slipping in at the back, a felt hat pulled down tightly about her, collar turned up so that she felt, in many ways, anonymous. Soon she was going every Sunday and sometimes during the week, a time she liked best of all because there so few there that it seemed like God must be in position to take more notice of her. And she began to talk to Him, awkwardly at first — it had been so long since she had made any attempt to communicate with Him — but with increased ease and confidence as the months went on.

Her hair grew again — a sign of new life, surely? And she even put on a little weight. She went back to work too, short days at first, then gradually building up. Life, it seemed, was destined to go on and inside her the feeling of peace grew also.

It was less than a year after her operation when they told her that the cancer had spread. Strangely, this time the fear of the future was less intense. Another operation followed, a lot more pain, another course of chemotherapy. Her hair fell out again and seemed reluctant to grow anew. Talking to one of the priests in the parish church where she was now a regular attender, she told him that she no longer felt afraid of death. The peace of God's love that had grown in her over the past year was strong enough to combat any fear.

She was tired, though, unable to sleep at night as pain took its hold on her wasting body. The family were devastated and Ruth found the roles reversed, as this time she was the one to comfort and console.

"I think I had accepted everything that was happening to me," she recalls.

"Although they tried to hide it from me at first, it was obvious that the cancer had now taken a grip and the future held no hope of recovery. I told my family that I just wanted to make the most of the time I had left with them.

"Then, just when it seemed that we had reached the darkest moment in our lives, another and to me even more terrible event took place. I had always relied on the support of my husband. Tom is one of those great gentle silent men, a foil for my volatile and hyperactive personality. We had two children, aged fourteen and seventeen. My greatest comfort was knowing that while they might miss me dreadfully, Tom would always be a rock in their lives. But one evening, we suffered a really devastating blow.

"Tom came home from work a little earlier than usual. He hadn't been feeling too good all afternoon, he said. In fact, he hadn't been feeling too good for a couple of weeks, tired, unwilling to eat, complaining now and then of a tingling and almost painful sensation in both arms and across his chest. I had asked him to go to our doctor, but he said he had probably been overdoing it and all he needed was a lazy weekend.

"He went to lie on the bed and shortly after I heard a thud. When I ran into the bedroom he was lying on the floor, one side of his face twisted. We called an ambulance and I went with him to the hospital, shaking all over.

"He'd had a stroke. One side of his body had been affected. They hoped for an improvement within forty-eight hours.

"Well, the improvement came, but not a total return to health. Tom's speech was affected, as was his right arm and leg. He was totally frustrated by being even semi-helpless, mainly, I suspected, because he knew that both I and the kids needed him so much right now."

Back home again, Tom and Ruth tried to pick up the pieces of life. It wasn't easy, especially when the children were unable to hide their fear of the future, that they would be left totally alone.

One day, Ruth noticed a hand-written sign in the church porch, inviting those who wished to join a local group travelling to New Orleans for a special healing service. The celebrant at the Mass was a Fr Peter Rookey. Ruth had heard of him. A friend who had been to Chicago to visit some friends had gone to a healing Mass there, and had come back enraptured with the priest and the powerful gift of healing that he undoubtedly had.

People had left their wheelchairs, she said, and pushed them down the aisle of the church. Others, when blessed by Fr Rookey had fallen back, to be caught before they hit the ground, then left there as if asleep while the healing ministry went on around them. Fr Rookey had called this 'resting in the spirit', Ruth was told, a 'beautiful meeting with God' was how he had described it. And people had been healed that night, her friend told her, without any doubt.

Could the priest heal Tom, she wondered suddenly? If only Tom could return to his full health, then she could die knowing that her children were in safe hands. But Tom wouldn't go, he said when she approached him about the Mass. He hadn't been to Mass since their youngest daughter was born. He saw no reason to go now. A God of love, as Ruth professed to believe in, wouldn't visit so many tragedies on the one family. And from that decision she had been unable to move him.

Calling up her friend on the telephone, Ruth asked how she could persuade Tom to change his mind.

"Don't even try," had been the advice.

"Go yourself. When we were at the healing Mass, Fr Rookey said that if we wished we could stand in for a blessing for somebody else. Why not just go and stand in for Tom?"

So she had done just that.

The coach trip to New Orleans tired her out physically, but the atmosphere was such that spiritually she felt invigorated. They had prayed the Rosary, then somebody had taken the microphone and read out what he called the 'Miracle Prayer' advocated by Fr Rookey for all who sought healing for themselves or others. Ruth repeated the words, mentally taking Tom and placing him at the foot of the cross of Christ.

It had been raining in New Orleans and the air smelled damp as Ruth left the coach, joining the crowds who were making their way into the church. Inside, the building was almost full although the Mass was not due to start for another thirty minutes. And because it was so crowded, stewards ushered the newcomers to single seats left vacant. Ruth found herself just three rows from the front, balanced at the end of a seat with a perfect view of the altar. In front of the first row were several wheelchairs, some of the people sitting in them looking beyond any help that man could give, Ruth thought. She felt unwell herself, but as the choir began to sing and the Rosary began, the discomfort of the journey was forgotten and she felt full of peace that she had come to pray for Tom's healing.

It was a beautiful Mass, she recalls. Simple, direct, just like the priest who celebrated it. Fr Rookey was older than she thought he would be, yet seemed full of energy and good humour, even throwing in a few jokes here and there, as he explained to those present what format the evening would take. First Mass, followed by blessing and anointing with holy oil. And, just as she'd been told, he emphasised the fact that it was possible for those there to 'stand in' for others who needed a blessing, but who could not be there.

"I felt very peaceful all night and very convinced that I was there for a reason, that Tom would indeed be healed. I felt particularly peaceful after receiving Communion, which I offered up for Tom's healing in spirit and body.

"Then came the healing part of the service. Stewards allowed us up, row by row. Just as I had been told, miraculous healings seemed to take place. A woman who was in a wheelchair stood up when Fr Peter invited her to take a step in faith with the Lord. Then she walked across the front of the altar and returned to push away her wheelchair. I think it was her daughter who was with her, and she was both laughing and crying at the same time. Then a man stepped out of his wheelchair and also pushed it down the aisle of the church. The whole congregation clapped him, and he looked so happy."

When it was her turn to move up to the front of the altar, Ruth felt suddenly very nervous. What if all this was just hysteria, unreal? What if she had come all this way for nothing? She remembers stopping suddenly so that the person behind bumped into her, wishing that she could just return to her seat, or preferably to the coach to wait there until this whole thing was over.

A gentle push from behind persuaded her to go forward. And as she stood in line in front of the altar, all her fears vanished.

"I was standing facing right towards the Tabernacle, and I felt as if Jesus was telling me it was all right to be there. Isn't that strange? I had never felt like this before.

"Fr Rookey moved along the line to my right, coming closer and as he did I looked straight at the Tabernacle and I gave all Tom's illness and fears to the Lord.

"I remember Fr Rookey stopping in front of me. He seemed to look straight into my eyes as I heard myself telling him that I had come to pray for my husband who'd had a stroke, and who had lost his faith in Jesus. Then he placed his hands on my head and made the sign of the cross on my forehead before blessing me again with a crucifix he held in his hand. Again I felt his hands gently on my head, and I heard him asking God to heal my husband and to bless me greatly and reward me for my love for my family.

"I'm not quite sure how to explain what happened next, but it was as if a wave of heat went right through my body, beginning at my head and going right down to my toes. That was the sensation, anyway. And I felt myself moving back through the air, not really falling, but as if I was gently going down and I had neither the wish nor the ability to stop myself.

"I remember the vague feeling of hands behind me, lowering me to the ground and I remember lying there, awake yet not awake, aware of what was going on round me, but as if it was not really around me. And I felt an experience of total and utter peace that I have never felt before or since in my life. It really was a meeting with God, and I will never be afraid of facing that God, who I now know is total and utter love. I felt loved and cared for and utterly peaceful and warm, and without any inclination to move or to 'return' to the outer world, as it then seemed to me to be."

Eventually, she says, she knew in herself that it was time to rejoin that world and the limbs which had seemed to melt into the ground now resumed movement. Hands helped her to her feet. Returning to her seat, feeling strangely drowsy and peaceful, she realised a little later that she had been some time lying there — about fifteen minutes, the woman beside her whispered as Ruth looked at her watch, wondering what time she had walked up to the altar.

The journey home seemed shorter. When she arrived, Tom was waiting for her, concerned that she had undertaken a journey that would have proved too strenuous for her frail body. And together, they sat on the couch, Ruth held in his arms, while she told him about the evening.

There seemed no obvious physical improvement in him she thought, but the anger had left him and wasn't that a healing? When they went to bed, they slept in each others arms until the sun beating on the window woke them almost nine hours later.

Tom's condition improved from that day, Ruth says. Slowly, but very surely, he regained the greater use of his right arm and his leg improved so that soon he walked with only a limp. It was the best he may get, the doctors told them when he went back for a check-up. Not a complete recovery, but good nonetheless and continued physiotherapy could bring about further improvement.

Ruth thanked God on the way home, and breathed a silent prayer for the black-robed priest who was surely the instrument of His healing in a world so much in need of healing. Not a day passed now, but she said the Miracle Prayer which had been handed out on cards in the church porch on the night of that healing Mass. Whatever the future held, however little time she had left, she felt at peace, her only wish that life could have been different and she could have lived to see her children grow and go on to lead their own lives. But God was undoubtedly good, and she had so much to be thankful for.

It was some time before she realised that she felt better than she had for many months. A remission, her family doctor told her. Time to enjoy her family. Two months later she returned to the hospital for tests and one week afterwards attended her specialist for a consultation.

"I remember that he looked at me strangely, when I went into his room," she says. "When he stood up to shake hands with me, he seemed to give me a very long questioning look. I remember my stomach seemed to turn over. He had obviously had bad results in the tests.

"I forced myself to sit quietly as he shuffled papers on his desk. I remember holding my hands tightly together, so they would not be seen shaking. Finally, he looked across at me, and I realised that he didn't quite know what to say to me, what words to use. I began to shake, and he reached across the desk to place his hands over mine as they lay on top of the desk.

"His words, when they came, were hesitant. The tests had shown up an unusual improvement in my condition. The cancer was there, but appeared more contained. They would like to do more tests."

The second tests, Ruth was told, were almost clear. Obviously, they said, the chemotherapy had been extremely effective in her case.

She was overjoyed going home. All that treatment had been worth it, even if the good results had come much later than expected. And then it hit her. She remembers stopping the car, pulling in to the side of the road, a strange warm feeling going through her as the thought struck her.

How could it have been the chemotherapy? How come they had given her no hope, no sign of improvement following the last course of treatment? And why had the doctor been so unusually inarticulate in dealing with her on the last two visits.

"And then it really hit me," she says. I had gone seeking healing for Tom and God had worked two miracles. He had healed both of us — Tom, whom I had prayed so desperately for and myself for whom I hadn't prayed at all because I had accepted that I was dying.

"And I just sat there, alone in my car at the side of the road, and I cried and cried and I laughed and then I cried again.

"And as long as I live, I will never cease to pray for Fr Peter Rookey.

"I remember what he said that night, that he was 'nothing but a rookie priest', that he could do nothing, but God could do everything. All he did was pray, he said.

"And I was left wondering, does he know just how successful his prayers are?"

Chapter Four

PRAYER AND FASTING

"The trouble with this world today," says Fr Peter, reaching under his black robe to pull out a worn handkerchief and wipe away the tiny mist of heat from his face, "is that it's success geared.

"We want success, and if possible instant success. And that works for our prayers too it seems.

"But the Lord did not call us to succeed. He called us to *try* to succeed and to be faithful in trying to succeed. The success, though, is His. As one of the Psalms says, the Lord gives success to the work of our hands.

"We have nothing to lose when we do not see an apparent success, because we are succeeding simply by being faithful to trying to succeed.

"So it is with praying. As we pray, we are being formed into the image and likeness of God. So we have nothing to lose. By our praying, the Lord is giving us a great desire to be healed of our cancer, or whatever we have and it doesn't matter in a sense whether we are healed physically, because by our praying we are being healed and prepared for heaven.

"Not only that, but we are being given a beauty treatment, because a person who is prayerful can not hide that. It's painted on their faces, a beauty and serenity, just as the unfortunate alcoholic or drug addict can not hide their problem. Whatever my problem, it comes out in my countenance, but when we pray we are enriched and enhanced, we become ever more beautiful until we die and then of course we receive the immortal beauty."

His relationship with Jesus and Mary is painted on his own face which despite travel and tiredness and an often too-heavy workload shows a serenity that surely goes beyond this world.

His entire life is a prayer, not just the three hours he devotes each day to talking with his Lord. Everything he does springs from a deep joy and belief in God, to whom he has given his entire life. Unfailingly good-humoured and ready at any opportunity to laugh and joke, no matter how long or how arduous the day has been, he takes each day as it comes, trusting in God to give him the strength to do whatever he is called upon to do.

His schedule is a demanding one, his monthly calendar marked out with only a day here and there not allocated to travelling, to attending healing Masses right across the United States and beyond.

Yet, few realise that this schedule is maintained on a strict diet of prayer and fasting, that this man of God, now well over the three score years and ten mark, eats just one meal a day and that generally close to midnight, after his healing Mass.

He's reluctant to discuss the subject. It's a personal arrangement between himself and his God, but when pressed attempts to pass it off as if he is only one among many in living this way.

"Oh well, this is just one of the things that the Lord seems to have given me, by some thought or action. He has put it upon me to fast every day and especially when I have a healing Mass to celebrate. And since I have a healing Mass most evenings, it's become a habit and I automatically don't eat until late at night. Although sometimes I do cheat a little and take a little coffee or tea or water," he says with a little shake of the head at his own apparent weakness.

But is it right to fast like this, I ask him? Can he physically have the strength to do all that he's doing while fasting so rigorously?

"Oh yes," he laughs, waving his hand as if to dismiss any notion of weakness.

"To the contrary, I feel better when I don't eat."

So does he believe that God is giving him the health and strength he needs?

"I'm quite sure He's doing that, because normally a person living an active or busy life needs at least some little thing to eat during the day, but I don't feel the need.

"And yet, you know, I have a great appetite, but I just say no to the food and I seem to get better mileage out of dear old Brother Ass this way, as St Francis called his body.

"They have this story, that when he was dying — St Francis — he turned to his Brother Ass and begged his pardon for treating him so poorly, because you know he fasted and flagellated his body so much."

It's been some years since he began this routine of strict fasting.

"Don't forget that in Medjugorje Our Lady asked for prayer and fasting and said that we could achieve miracles with these two powerful spiritual weapons. There she asks for the bread and water fast on at least two days a week, Wednesday and Friday, but I guess that maybe because I'm a bigger sinner the Lord put it to me to fast every day, although I do eat one meal at night.

"And sometimes I wonder," he says, a deep questioning look in his eyes, "if He means me to go without eating altogether and gain all my strength from the Eucharist, as did Teresa Neumann."

His belief in the presence and power of Jesus in the Eucharist is total. It's the cornerstone of our faith, he says, and if we need any proof to believe that the body and blood of the Risen Christ is present in the Eucharist we celebrate, then we have it in the many Eucharistic miracles that have occurred.

"Take the miracle of the Eucharist that happened at Lanciano in Italy, for example," he says.

"We were there about a year ago and witnessed the proof for ourselves. It's a miracle that occurred in the 8th century and is still there to see today.

"It happened when a priest who was experiencing doubts in his faith and particularly in relation to the Real Presence of Christ in the Eucharist, pronounced the words all priests say at the Consecration. 'This is my body', he said, holding up the bread and as he did so the Host turned into flesh, and blood dropped into the chalice beneath.

"And that piece of flesh can be seen to this day, preserved in a glass tabernacle. When tested, it was proved to be a piece of human heart tissue. Even the length of time that it has been preserved is a miracle in itself. And there have been many other miracles of the Eucharist, which God has permitted so that our weak faith could be strengthened."

He has had his own experiences of miraculous proof in the Real Presence of Jesus in the Eucharist, he continues.

On many occasions in recent years, he has seen Jesus in the Host as he pronounces the Consecration.

"Unworthy as I am, it has been a great source of strength to me," he says simply, as he recalls the times when holding up the Host, he has seen the face of Christ in it.

It's the Eucharist from which he gets his strength, undoubtedly, he says.

"That and Our Blessed Lady through whom Jesus came to us," he continues.

His devotion to Mary is deeply founded in his upbringing, he admits. His mother had a great devotion to the Mother of God and passed this on to her family. It was one of the reasons why, in time, he came to join the Servants of Mary and also why he invokes the intercession of the Virgin at every Mass and during his healing prayers.

He was touched by an account given to him by a Chicago woman who attended his fiftieth celebrations at the Basilica of Our Lady of Sorrows on May 26th 1991. Only three priests from his class remained to celebrate their Golden anniversary, Fr Peter, Fr Philip Brennan and Fr Dominic Manzo.

The Mass began with the procession of priests from the Basilica, followed by the three anniversary celebrants who took their places on the altar. Fr Rookey took his place on the right side of the altar, facing the congregation.

Following Communion, Rose Johnson, looking up at the altar from her place on the right of the Basilica, suddenly saw the image appear of a Lady behind the right shoulder of Fr Peter. She wore a white veil and a blue bodice, Rose recalls clearly. The veil blew gently around her and her hands were by her side. When the congregation were asked to applaud the three priests who had given fifty years each to the service of Jesus and Mary, Fr Peter turned slightly to his right and bowed, directly it seemed to Rose Johnson, to the Lady who held out her hands to him exactly as a gentle loving mother does to embrace her child. Fr Rookey's hand was raised to the altar as he bowed for the second time.

"Anybody who has ever known Fr Rookey would know that this was his way of saying that all the praise being given belonged to Jesus and Mary," Rose explained afterwards.

"When he bowed in such deep humility, I thought perhaps he had seen Our Lady too. Later I realised that I had been the only one, as far as I was aware, to witness this tender moment between Our Mother and her son."

A real experience, or one simply imagined during the emotion of the event?

Humbled and deeply touched as he was by the account and the thought that the Mother of God, whom he carries in his heart, had favoured him with so great an honour, Fr Peter had no problem accepting it.

"Rose Johnson is a beautiful and inspired person," he says.

"She is well educated and has great faith. I have no reason to disbelieve what she says.

"At the moment when she says she saw Mary, I was turning to Jesus on the cross and the words on my lips were, 'Not to us, oh Lord, but to your name be the glory'.

"I don't feel comfortable, you know, with applause and praise because I know how great a sinner I am and how I can do nothing, that it is the Lord who does everything.

"Strangely, and what is interesting, is that an artist who lives in London painted a picture of me shortly afterwards. He had no knowledge of this happening with Rose Johnson in Chicago, but when he came to paint the picture he depicted me with my ear cocked to Our Lady, while I bless a little boy with the cross in my hand. When Rose later saw this, she said that it was very similar to the vision she'd had at the Golden Jubilee."

Chapter Five

NO THOUGHT OF HEALING

'Dear Fr Rookey,

My story is very involved, but I am writing to let you know that I have been truly touched by Jesus.

For two years I had suffered from tremendous head pain. I finally found a doctor who would listen and would hang in there with me. My doctor ordered an MRI which showed a shadow that the doctors thought was a vascular mass. They then ordered an artiography which showed that I had a small benign tumour.

They called in a surgeon who told me I would probably not survive the surgery, that the least I could hope for was to be left blind and paralysed; or that I would end up in a vegetative state. We made arrangements for me to be in the hospital for twelve to fourteen weeks and then to go to live for a while at a rehabilitation centre. Breaking this to my two small children was frightening.

Before surgery, the doctors got very angry with me because I told them that Jesus would not desert me and that I would be fine. They told us that the surgery would be three and a half hours. It ended up being seven and a half hours. When they opened me up they said I should have been dead months before. My brain was so swollen that it was starting to disintegrate and I had a tumour twice the size the test had showed. Plus, it was wrapped round the brain stem. They were later astounded that I could talk, recognise people and wiggle my fingers and toes.

I lay on the critical list for three days. Unknown to me at this time, you came in. My girlfriend had gone to see you and told you she had a friend who just underwent brain surgery, but we did not know if it was cancer yet. You told her it was, but that I would be cured. She then stood in for a proxy blessing for me. She said that before she went down, her head burned and felt like it had cracked in three places (everywhere I was cut). Then you told her to go to the hospital and lay her hands on my head and say the Miracle Prayer. She did as you said and I made a turn for the better the next day and was out of 'neuro' in a week and a half.

I am fine today. I wanted to take this opportunity to thank you for helping to cure and heal me through the help of Jesus. I end this letter to you in the way that I end all of my prayers daily.

May Jesus forever live in my heart, be the sounds in my ears, the words on my lips and the lamplights of my eyes.

Fondly yours in Christ.' (Ohio)

It's mid-March in Chicago, just a couple of days past Saint Patrick's day and the weather is as inclement as if it was still mid-winter.

Fr Peter edges his car forward, a padded jacket over his black robe and a fur hat on his head, flaps hanging loose over his ears. Slowing now and then to wipe the windscreen with a rag, he peers through the glass as the snow blizzards down all around him, blowing freely through the partly opened window and covering the passengers with icy wetness.

"Cold? Not at all," he argues.

"You'd want to grow up on Lake Superior to know what cold is. Down there everybody tries to organise their vacation during the forty-eight hours of summer!" he laughs.

The car is typical of the unworldly character of the man who drives it. Old and small, it seems to have been invented before effective heaters were thought of.

David Parkes pulls the collar of his jacket closer round his ears, declines the laughing offer of an old blanket in the back seat to raise his body temperature and attempts to help Fr Peter find his way through the blizzard.

A sudden chill runs down his back, causing him to shiver noticeably.

"Somebody walk over your grave?" Fr Peter asks quizzically.

David shakes his head in denial, thinking to himself how apt the question was.

Turning to look at the smiling face of the priest seated beside him, he involuntarily places a hand on Fr Peter's shoulder in a gesture of love and gratitude.

If it wasn't for this great and humble man of God, he reminds himself, he would be — where? He didn't have an answer to that one. Where did people go after death when they turned their backs on God? To a spiritual wilderness, at best he imagined.

Fr Peter reached up to lay his own hand firmly on the hand that David seemed unable to remove from his shoulder, and at the touch of the priest's firm grasp David found it difficult to hold back the tears of emotion that threatened to spill down his face.

He owed everything to this man. Both his physical healing and, even more, his spiritual rebirth.

Sitting in the quietness of the car, the loudest sounds being the laboured clicking of the windscreen wipers, he thought how strange it was to be here in Chicago with the man he credited with the saving of his life.

He remembered the first time he met Fr Rookey. It was at Dublin airport on the way to Medjugorje, Bosnia-Herzegovina of all places. He weighed roughly nine stone then, a long way from the fourteen stone he put up on the scales these days.

Huddled in a leather jacket, he had done his best to avoid talking to the priest who was to be Spiritual Director for the pilgrimage to the valley where for the past eight years the Virgin Mary had been reported to appear daily to a group of young local people.

The other one hundred and sixty six passengers may be going on a pilgrimage, he snapped to his wife Anne, but he certainly wasn't. The only reason he had agreed to come at all was because some well-meaning people had decided that if he went he would be healed, and had given himself and Anne the tickets as a gift.

And besides, the week's trip to the country where he and Anne had spent their honeymoon could be seen as a few days convalescence.

He could do with that, he knew. The illness that had dogged him for the past twelve years had just about reached the end of its course. After ten major operations and every type of drug possible, the medical people had admitted that there was nothing more they could do to combat the severe bowel disease from which he suffered.

The future? They had refused to answer that one and their silence said more than any words.

Looking with affection at the man now sitting beside him, he remembered the first time he had heard his name. Ironically, it was at a cabaret function to raise money for his family, as he thought, who were suffering very badly financially as a result of his inability to work in recent months. A professional singer and big band leader, his world had been turned upside down by the illness that had eaten into his life for so many years.

He'd come a long way downhill over those years. Once a professional footballer for some of Ireland's best known teams, he had later moved into show business full time after winning a national talent contest, chucking in his secure job as a department store buyer and public relations manager.

It was a long time later when his friends told him that the fund-raising event, in a large Dublin hotel and attended by many of the country's leading entertainers, was in fact to raise the money needed to pay his funeral expenses. Nobody had thought that he would live much longer.

They'd asked him to sing that night and he had, despite the fact that his stomach muscles had been cut to pieces. And later in the night had come the offer to travel to Medjugorje with a Fr Peter Rookey.

He kept as far as possible from the priest in the airport lounge, mentally cursing the tour organiser who kept trying to get them together. And even in Medjugorje he did his best to avoid the black-robed priest who was surrounded by crowds wherever he went. He planned to go to Dubrovnik the next day, he told Anne, check into a decent hotel and get as far away from this religious hysteria as possible.

Reluctantly, he allowed her to persuade him 'for decency's sake' to attend just one of the priest's so-called healing services after morning Mass, down in the local cemetery behind the church of St James. And with even greater reluctance he finally agreed to heed her continuous pleading to stand in line to receive a blessing. That done, he whispered to her, he was leaving, if he had to walk all the way to Dubrovnik.

One thing was certain, he told himself as the priest moved along the line and closer to him, he would not succumb to the mass hysteria that was prevailing in the cemetery, as people fell backwards to lie motionless on the ground when the priest gave them his blessing. His body may be wasted, but nobody — and he meant nobody, not even this black-robed Servite — was going to push him down.

He had handed Anne the video camera he had borrowed to take with him on the trip when he went to join the line. And despite the fact that she had never worked a cam-corder before in her life, she somehow managed to record the entire event.

First another priest, assisting the Servite, blessed him then passed on by. He felt no particular sensation at all.

Moments later the black-robed figure was standing in front of him.

What did he wish to pray for? How did he know, he wondered, then heard himself telling the priest that he'd had several major operations recently, and didn't feel at all well.

The priest had blessed him then, anointing him with holy oil before placing in his hands the old worn crucifix he carried. David remembered Fr Peter taking the cross from his hands as a strange sensation of heat ran through his entire body.

And after that, nothing — until he found himself looking up from the red earth where he had lain, they later told him, for almost twenty minutes.

There had been no thought of healing in his mind as somebody helped him to his feet. Only a sheepish feeling that he must have looked ridiculous lying there for so long. What had happened? He wasn't sure. The first thought in his mind, in fact, was had somebody hit him?

It was twenty-four hours later before he realised that for the first time in years he was experiencing none of the debilitating symptoms of the disease. No nausea, pain or vomiting. No weakness, he realised. And he was standing straight... and he felt strong enough to climb the mountains, which he did later in the week.

The tests, when he returned to his doctors some weeks later, showed a massive improvement in the disease. Later tests could find no symptoms and while a huge part of his bowel was missing due to the operations, he had experienced no signs of the illness over the last five years.

A miraculous cure? There was no other explanation, he told himself, although he would have been the last to have believed it of anybody else.

But, more than the physical healing which was so great in itself he had, during that week in Medjugorje in the company of Fr Peter, experienced a genuine spiritual healing that had remained with him ever since.

He knew he would never be able to repay the priest for his prayer. These days, he didn't even attempt to. Fr Peter had made it clear on more than one occasion that the healing was none of his doing, that all of the glory and the praise for it must go to Jesus, who had reached out in love to hand him back his life.

As the car pulled into the grounds of a church in an outlying district of Chicago, David looked at the people who already, an hour before the designated time for the Mass, were making their way into the building.

Miracles could — and did — happen, he told himself. And later, he told the congregation gathered there the same thing, as Fr Peter invited him to tell his story so that all would know the greatness and the power of God's love.

And he sang for them, his voice clear and strong with, he knew, a new depth of emotion that he had noticed since the healing. The *Ave Maria*, in honour of the Blessed Mother who had undoubtedly led him to her Son, through this other son who sat close to him on the altar. And then, the song that he had recorded in thanksgiving for his healing.

It was 1989 when he had first gone to Medjugorje. At every Mass, American pilgrims requested prayers for those in their country who were legislating on the abortion laws.

Standing on top of Podbrdo, the hill where the Virgin Mary had first appeared to the young visionaries, he had made a promise to record a song he had been given years before, but which had never seen the light of day since.

Let Me Live, it was called, a song of the pre-born child begging for the right to experience life. He dedicated it to his own son Kenneth who had been born with cystic fibrosis, for which a foetus could now be tested and if discovered the pregnancy terminated.

Kenneth was eighteen now. He'd been through some rough times and the future was uncertain. Another time, in another place, he might never have been allowed live and yet, over those eighteen years he had brought a wealth of love into the family.

As the last note died away there was a moment of hushed silence before the congregation, many of them in tears, rose to their feet to applaud.

Standing there, tears in his own eyes, David felt a hand on his shoulder and turned to be gripped in the arms of Fr Peter.

"Thank you, thank you," murmured the priest.

"No," David replied, clutching the priest in a bear-like hug. "Thank you — for everything."

Chapter Six

CASTING OUT DEMONS

'Dear Fr Rookey,

I am writing this letter to testify to God's power and His Mother's love for all of us. May the hearts of Jesus and Mary be praised!

I am 21 years old. Since late 1987, I had been suffering from a chronic depressive state. For the first couple of years it was manageable, but by the beginning of 1990 it was so severe that it rendered me dysfunctional for almost two years until January 20th, 1992. It was on this day that God chose to liberate me from the hands of despair.

Although I had suffered many difficult experiences in my life, this prolonged depression was an absolute hell on wheels. I constantly prayed to Our Lady for deliverance and when I received a letter from the Messengers of Mary saying that you were going to be at Our Lady of Mount Carmel in Doyleston, PA on January 20th, 1992, I knew that Our Lady and providence had reserved my healing for that day, because I had been born on the feast day of Our Lady of Mount Carmel and I had a devotion to St John Neuman who had founded the church building itself.

After having gone to confession, I prayed the Rosary then went to Communion. While kneeling and thanking God for the grace of having been able to attend the healing service, I began to get a strong inner sense of peace that no matter what would happen at the healing service, whether I was healed or not, I would be taken care of by the Lord.

With this in my heart I went up to the altar to be blessed by you, dear Father. I was one of the first people to be anointed in the whole church, which was packed. When you came up to me I said to myself that I was going to try not to fall, since I was intimidated by the idea. I had never been slain in the spirit before. Even though I resisted vigorously, when you said the final words of prayer I felt a wind flash by me and I could stand no longer.

As I remained on the floor I was not aware of time or space. I was very much at peace. When people would walk past me and their clothes would brush up against me, I remembered where I was. After about fifteen minutes or so I attempted to 'snap out of it' and get up with the help of my mother. As I sat up an overwhelming feeling of peace overtook me and I fell back on the floor again. This happened several times. By then, I realised that God wanted to work on me, so I let go.

I began receiving 'divine therapy' as I would see painful scenes from the past and I would feel God's love healing them. I began to cry uncontrollably. My whole body became warm. This went on for quite a while. My mother became very worried because of my loud and uncontrollable crying and she would try to make me get up again. It was useless.

I remember consciously hearing the people gathering around me after the healing service was over. Then I realised that I had to get up. The more I would try to get up, the more I would feel forced back to the floor. I became very anxious and embarrassed in front of the gathering crowd.

Father, you then came to me and began praying over me. At first everything was fine. All of a sudden, I began feeling very sick physically. I felt something coming over me in waves. My body began to contort uncontrollably. My tongue started coming out of my mouth and my eyes would roll back. At all times, the people around me would pray.

When I became more aware of what was happening, I would panic because I could see my mother crying, then I would go out again. Father, you then blessed me over and over again with your cross. An anger would well up in me and I would scream wildly.

By now, whenever I would come to I would start thinking that this whole thing was a dream. It was too scary and awful to be real. The people round me made me drink holy water in these lucid moments; then I would start throwing up the holy water and cursing.

I don't like to say I did these things, because my will was to stop them from happening, but they were really uncontrollable.

By now, some hours had gone by and this ordeal was not ending. All I wanted to do was to get up and go home. I would start crying before this 'devil' would take over again and cause me to be violent. At one point, when the devil was getting weaker, I would find that I could control my legs, but my arm was still being controlled by this magnetic force. That is the best way to describe it. It was as if there were a field of magnetism gluing me to the floor and forcing my hand to make a fist and swing at you, Father.

At times when I would really go under its control, I would start spitting at you and the cross. When I fully realised this, I would fight even harder to stop these things from happening. At one point I actually thought it was not going to end.

But thank God, you persevered and the oppression lessened. All in all it took approximately three and a half hours for me to come out of being slain in the spirit totally.

When I was going home I could actually sense a big change for the better in my emotional health. I felt unburdened and relieved.

Upon your advice, I went to see you again the next day, Tuesday, January 21st, 1992 at St Vincent Palotti Church in Hatboro, NJ. All day long my family and I prayed for a sign that I had truly and fully been delivered.

After Communion, my face and hands began to burn and I felt as if I was going to collapse on the pew during the final last minutes of the Mass. I knew in my heart that I shouldn't fear because God would once again prove His love for me.

When I went up to the altar, I stood beneath the statue of Our Lady and begged her for a sign that the grace had been fully granted and that I had nothing to fear as far as any recurrence of the demonic influence on me. A few seconds after making this petition, a burst of fragrant roses broke out. It was very intense. I knew that was Our Lady telling me I would be all right.

When you came up to me Father, you immediately recognised me and you prayed intensely over me. I was slain only after repeated prayers on your part and the application of the Blessed Cross to my forehead. This night though, I arose seconds after being slain. You prayed over me again after I stood up, but nothing would happen. I then smelled the roses again! The grace had been granted — I was all right.

It has been almost a month since I was delivered from demonic oppression and my psychological state has improved drastically. I believe that Our Lady is healing me according to God's schedule. My concentration and mood have improved very much. I can get by day after day now without a constant sense of despair. I do believe that when the evil spirit(s) was/were exorcised, my mind was allowed to heal. The Lord knows what He's doing, and I praise Him and thank Him and His Mother for having sent you to me.

Ave Maria and God bless you,

Love, S.

"We're all attacked constantly by evil spirits," Fr Peter explains.

The evening traffic in Chicago is densely packed as we make our way into the city. Father Peter winds his way expertly through it, lane-hopping where necessary, seemingly unconcerned by the hampered movement, while the faces of others, caught in the ongoing stream of cars on their way home from a day's work, show signs of tension and frustration.

We've been sitting in traffic for well over an hour now, yet it hasn't seemed so long. Already, we've said two Rosaries, the general prayer that most people say and the Seven Dolours of Our Lady so loved by the Servants of Mary.

Just the evening before there'd been an example of demonic possession during one of Fr Peter's healing Masses. It wasn't the first exorcism I'd seen him perform, but an experience like that is not one you ever grow used to and I still felt chilled by the experience.

"Some of those evil spirits are invited in by activities such as ouija boards, the occult and all that entails — the giving of ourselves to the devil and such like. Others are visited upon us by the intentions of others."

And yet, he continues, when he looks back over his long years in the healing ministry and those healings that have left a special mark on him as signs of God's great power, he has to admit that the exorcisms come immediately to mind.

One of these occurred in Atlanta, Georgia where a teenage girl was brought to him by her desperately anxious parents.

"The father was Jewish and the mother Catholic," he recalls.

"The girl herself had become involved with the occult and had gone so far as to give herself to Wicca, the witch, for powers that she proudly extolled to me. She was bragging about these powers and so I challenged her. I asked whether she was willing to pit Wicca's powers against those of Jesus Christ. But she said, 'Oh no, I am happy with the powers she gives me,' and no matter how I tried to persuade her, she wouldn't budge from that. Eventually she burst into tears and left us and went out to sit in her parent's car.

"I went out to say goodbye to her when they were leaving. I wanted to keep friendly toward her and not have her go away angry, you know.

"Well," he continues, once again manoeuvring the car through the traffic, this time to make his way onto an exit lane, "the next time I was in Atlanta I found that the father and mother, who wanted her to be delivered from this so badly, had put her into a mental institution with very high level psychological and medical help. So high-level in fact, that it cost a thousand dollars a week to maintain her there.

"I went to visit her, this time at the invitation of the girl herself who, I reckon, wanted to get out of that palace, as nobody likes to be in these institutions no matter how expensive they might be.

"Whatever her motivation, and I don't want to judge that, she was open to exorcism this time. I wasn't so sure that the clinic staff would be so open, mind you.

"A very tall lady doctor allowed us in to see her, I recall, but made sure to stand just outside the door for a while to see what this rookie priest was going to get up to. I guess she was satisfied after a while, because we were just praying and asking the Lord to deliver this child, so she left."

The exorcism took some time, he recalls, but the powers of Wicca proved pitiful against the almighty power of Jesus Christ.

"By the end she had shown all the signs of deliverance and before I left she asked that we all say a Rosary together. Now things have turned round completely in her life and her boy friend, who was into this Wicca thing with her, has also turned around and now they go to Mass together and practice their faith."

There have been other exorcisms, too many to recall them all, in every part of the world to which he has travelled.

The young girl he met in Medjugorje, Bosnia-Herzegovina, for example, who had been cursed by her grandmother.

"She turned out to have five demons in her," Fr Peter continues, pulling up at the lights beside a large open car with a group of young teenagers whose stereo is turned up so high they must all surely be unable to talk to each other. Fr Peter gives them a cheery wave of the hand.

"How are you doin'?" he asks and they wave to him in reply.

"God bless you now. You all take care, you hear?" he adds, making the sign of the cross in their direction before they drive away leaving us well in their wake.

"They gave her their names," he continues, as if the conversation had never been interrupted.

"The demons," he reminds me, seeing the puzzled expression on my face.

"I have them written down. One was Lucifer.

"She was Italian, a lovely girl. I still correspond with her and while she may have been delivered of these spirits, like all of us she is still being attacked by the forces of evil only in her case perhaps more than some of us, as these boys never like to lose a soul."

Why does it sometimes take more than one exorcism to banish the evil spirits, I ask, one incident clearly recalled in my mind from a healing service Fr Peter had performed in County Wicklow, Ireland.

"Oh, that's because the demons are very strongly entrenched and even in the time of Our Lord, this was no unusual happening.

"You recall the story of how the people brought a young man who was possessed to be exorcised by Jesus?

"The man who brought him said to the Lord: 'I brought him to your disciples, but they could not cast out the demon'. So Jesus took and cast him out and afterwards the disciples asked Jesus: 'Why could we not cast him out?' and Jesus replied, 'This kind can be cast out only by prayer and fasting.' So maybe they had not prayed and fasted enough, or whatever.

"This is one of the reasons, I expect, why the Lord has put it on me so strongly to add fasting to my prayer."

The sun streams in the car window, yet I can't help the shiver that goes through my body.

I can remember, vividly, the exorcism I have just called to Fr Peter's recollection, the first I had ever witnessed.

Fr Peter was in the middle of a two-week visit to Ireland, performing healing Masses every day in churches and halls throughout the country. One evening he attended a prayer meeting in a town in County Wicklow on Ireland's east coast. The small room was crowded with about fifty people who had come to pray with him and afterwards, he gave his blessing to each one, anointing them with the holy oil he carries everywhere.

Many of those who were blessed rested in the spirit, eventually being helped to their feet and returning to their seats with expressions of obvious peace written all over their faces. All through this, the entire group recited the Rosary, singing beautifully spiritual hymns between each decade. The feeling of love and joy in the room was tangible.

Only a few people remained to be blessed when my attention was suddenly drawn to a young man who had been lying on the floor for some time. Motionless before this, he now showed signs of some interior agitation, as he began to moan and to toss around on the hard wooden floor. Before long, the tossing had become much wilder as he thrashed about, shouting and banging the floor with his fists, though all the time lying on his back and moving about from side to side.

Fr Peter, who had come over to bless him a couple of times, an action that had given him some peace for a few minutes on each occasion, now turned to give him his full attention. Yet the more the priest prayed over him, the more violent the man became.

"Continue to pray," Fr Peter demanded, as the group fell silent mainly I suspect through fear, a fear which I had no problem admitting to myself. My many years as a journalist had brought me into varied and often difficult situations, particularly during the time I had spent in investigative work. But never had I felt such a strong sensation of fear as I now did in this room while an exorcism took place within only a few feet of me.

The entire group had now moved back as far as they could against the walls forming, strangely and without any intention, a circle round the two central figures in the drama. Time and time again Fr Peter, holding the cross in front of the young man's face, tried to break through the wall of evil.

"Look at your Saviour," he commanded. "Look into His face," but the possessed man struggled and writhed and closed his eyes tightly and refused to look at the crucifix.

Time seemed almost to stand still as again and again the black-robed priest, now down on the floor and leaning over the young man, sprinkled him with holy water, held the cross before his face and challenged the spirits who fought so hard to maintain their hold on his life.

"Who are you?" Fr Peter thundered at one stage. "Give me your name," and from the man's mouth in a snarling, strangled voice poured a string of names among which I heard the name 'Beelzebub'.

"In the name of Jesus Christ our Saviour, I command you to come out of this man," Fr Peter called in a loud, strong voice.

My skin felt icy with fear and the words of the Rosary being said around me refused to come out from my own lips for a few moments. Thoughts flashed rapidly across my mind. Would the spirits come out or would this go on for ever?

It was almost an hour now since the exorcism had begun.

And if and when they did come out, where would they go? The Gospel stories raced through my mind, the times that Jesus had cast out spirits and ordered them into nearby animals, like the swine that had fled possessed and thrown themselves into the lake.

Instinctively I held up the blessed cross that hung round my neck, in front of my face. Never before had I understood the expression about the hair standing up on the back of one's neck. Now I did.

The snarling and shouting of the man on the floor was not human, as again and again he tried to avoid complying with Fr Peter's demands, at times lashing out in an attempt to strike the priest, but always, strangely, missing.

"Say the name of Jesus," Fr Peter ordered in a voice so powerful it must surely have been heard on the street.

I felt my breath catching as the man continued to snarl and writhe.

Fr Peter repeated the command several times and suddenly, from the young man's lips was wrung a strangled version of the name. "Jesus".

"I don't hear you right," Fr Peter said to him in a loud voice. "Say the name of Jesus," the priest repeated.

"Jesus," the man moaned faintly, then again, in a stronger voice this time.

"Jesus, Jesus, Jesus..." he repeated, crying now, tears of relief and release as the powerful name of Jesus delivered him from his possession.

Afterwards, he sat quietly while Fr Peter talked to him, asking him to return to see him the following day.

It was an appointment he didn't keep, something that didn't seem to surprise Fr Peter.

Later that night, as he ate his one meal of the day, I asked Fr Rookey whether he believed the man had been truly liberated.

"That depends on a number of things," he replied. "Especially on his own determination to start afresh."

And the demons, I asked — those who had undoubtedly been forced from him — where did they go?

"Oh, you don't have to worry about them," Fr Peter laughed, seeing the concern on my face.

"I banished and bound them in the name of Jesus. They won't bother you."

It was about a year later when I heard of another exorcism in Ireland, this time in a town a little south of Wicklow. After a healing Mass, Fr Peter as usual blessed each individual who came up to him, many again resting in the spirit for what Father always describes as this beautiful meeting with Jesus.

Again, each person who lay peacefully on the church floor eventually rose to their feet and returned to their seats. Those helping them up suddenly became aware of one young man, still lying down, who was beginning to make 'snaking' movements as, on his back, he began to writhe and wriggle towards the front row of seats, an activity that increased dramatically when Fr Peter approached him. The exorcism that followed was just as dramatic as the one I had previously witnessed, but this time was lasting. The young man (and it was the same person from the previous year) returned to Fr Peter twice over the next days, received his blessing, rested in the spirit, then returned peacefully to his seat.

He had been somehow involved with others who had meddled with the occult, Fr Peter explained to me afterwards. And the evil spirits were reluctant to release him.

"If we open the door," Fr Peter repeated once more, "the old boy will come in. It doesn't take him long."

He recalls other incidences, like the house in Cleveland, Ohio where a murder had occurred and where, he says matter of factly, the evil spirits had been very strong but had also succumbed.

Then there was the time in Las Vegas where he carried out a healing Mass in an old casino on the Strip.

"That was a two-night stand," he recalls with a laugh.

"I always say now that I once played Las Vegas!"

He'd gone there on the invitation of the local bishop. The casino had been crowded for each Mass, a wonderful triumph Fr Peter reflected, of the things of God overruling the things of the world.

On the second night, a video was shown beforehand of the apparitions of the Mother of God in the world in recent years. Among the congregation was a young woman who watched the video and listened to the talk preceding Mass with interest, stayed for the Mass itself, but when it came time for the laying on of hands and the blessing of the sick, made a bee-line for the exit.

"She told us afterwards that when she got to the door, some unknown force pushed her back into the room," Fr Peter recalls.

"Again she tried to leave and again the same thing happened, so she gave up and stayed there.

"Eventually — and very unwillingly — she came up with a group of others to be blessed. As soon as I held my hand up over her, the old boy threw her down violently on the floor and she began growling and yelling and writhing around — all the usual signs of possession. So we prayed over her for some time and eventually that old boy just came out of her. And when the other people there had all been prayed with, she came back up for another blessing and this time she rested peacefully in the spirit, then got up and immediately gave a wonderful witness of her life and the experience she had just gone through."

Do you believe that you are truly being used as the hands of the Holy Spirit in all of these circumstances, I ask Fr Peter?

"Oh yes," he replies without hesitation, "just as a mother and father are the hands of the Lord in their families. And while mothers and fathers might not be perfect very often, we have to remember that before God we are all sinners. And God uses even sinners to carry out his work, of which I am one of the greatest, so it's not a question of our thinking that we're some great personage, or even just a little less than God, although the psalmist in Psalm Eight assures us of that very thing. No, but in this sense we do share in His godliness because according to the first chapter of Genesis, we are made in His image and likeness. Unfortunately, we lost that through sin and we became uglier. And the greater the sinner we are the uglier we become in our image.

"I see this very visibly when I am called upon to carry out exorcisms, when the demon makes the countenance of the person concerned so grotesque. Oh, it's like something right out of hell.

"And then, in contrast, after the person has been delivered, he has such a different and a beautiful countenance and bearing."

Does he ever experience fear during these exorcisms, I ask, remembering my own fear during the event I had witnessed?

"Well, not any more fear than the realisation I have all the time that, if we can believe Padre Pio as he was quoted as saying, there are more demons attacking us now than there are people who have been born since the beginning of our world.

"But the good news is that there are many more angels protecting us, so if we call on this protection we have nothing to fear.

"My greater fear is the constant one we all have, of offending God who has given us everything including life."

Chapter Seven

THROUGH OTHERS...

'Dear Fr Rookey,

I am writing this letter to tell you about the healing of my daughter. A few weeks ago she'd had pains and went to the doctor to have tests to see what the trouble was. She had three mammograms and two ultra sound tests. The doctor discovered there was a chance that the growth they found was partially malignant.

Being her mother I was very concerned, more so than my daughter who, being so young and so vibrant, continued to get up for work at three o'clock in the morning and to work for a full day.

So I stormed heaven, asking my prayer group to pray for her and also many other people. At your First Saturday service this December, Father, you asked for prayers for her and the hundreds of people there joined you in prayer. What power there is when people pray together! Also, two people stood in proxy for her so she received a double anointing. Her mother's tears watered the flowers of prayer and sent signals to the throne of the Almighty.

I can never thank you enough Father, for your concern, interest and prayer. The next Monday when she went back for another examination before surgery, the doctor exclaimed: 'It's gone!'

We call it a miracle. Praise the Lord. What a relief to know that my daughter is out of danger! Thank you Jesus, thank you Mary and all you angels and saints! And thank you again, Father.

What a wonderful Christmas gift!

Gratefully.' (Illinois)

Isn't it strange, I wonder aloud, that even without hands being laid on them, many sick people are healed through the love and prayers of others?

"Not in the slightest," Fr Peter replies as we sit on a wooden bench in the late afternoon sunshine.

"While the Lord told His disciples to go out into the world and lay their hands on people in His name and their ills would be healed and their demons cast out, His power is not restricted to touch."

But Father, I protest, yesterday I heard you praying over the telephone with people who were ill and I know from the letters that pour into your International Compassion Ministry that many people are healed in this way. And yet it's at such a distance, and there is no laying on of hands? How do you explain that?

"God's powers are not limited in any way by time or space," he replies with a smile, "as was witnessed in the Gospel when Jesus healed the servant of the centurian. When He told the officer that He would come and heal the man, the soldier replied: 'I am not worthy that You should come under my roof. But only say the word and he will be healed'. What faith that was. As Jesus said, He had never seen such faith, even in Israel, yet here was this pagan Roman officer expressing complete belief in His power to heal. And what did He do then? 'Be it done as you say,' Jesus said and at that moment the centurian's servant was healed.

"You know," he continues as a warm breeze blows about us, "I always tell mothers that their prayers are the most compelling and powerful for the flesh of their flesh, bone of their bone. There are so many examples in Christian history where a mother's prayers have obtained great graces and healing, as in the case of St Monica and St Augustine who we discussed previously.

"And again and again there are examples that when we stand in proxy for another person, or pray especially for another as was the case with the centurian, then that person is healed.

"Take the example of a young man in New Orleans about four years ago, who came to a healing Mass and stood in for his friend who was in a coma in a hospital in Louisiana. When he put together all the events afterwards, he discovered that the friend had come out of the coma at the same time that we were praying for him in the church.

"Then last year in Chicago arch-diocese in River Grove, a lady who lived across the road from the church came to the Mass and came up for a blessing for a man who was in a coma in the local hospital. After the healing she returned home, and soon after she arrived the telephone rang and they reported to her that the man had just come out of the coma."

'Dear Fr Rookey,

I took home one of your Miracle Prayer cards and read it over and over until I could feel that I meant every word I said. This is what happened to me.

For five years, since my husband died, my youngest daughter and I have had no relationship whatsoever. I was so angry with her because of the way she treated her father and me during his bout with cancer and even after his death.

She never came to console me or him. She would not even talk to us on the phone and believe that God could heal her Dad through their prayers. They never called to see how I was and accused me of talking and telling stories about them. So I was very angry and didn't see how I could ever forgive them for the way they treated my husband just before he passed away.

Anyway, after five years I prayed the Miracle Prayer and God has helped me to forgive them. Also, by a strange coincidence my daughter developed a lymph node infection (which she thought was cancer) and called me on the phone and asked me to go with her for the operation. I did, and it turned out to be just an infection, but that episode has brought us all back together. I can once again see my two grandchildren and enjoy my daughter and her family.

I firmly believe that this prayer plus many others I said were heard by God and has finally helped me to forgive them.

Thank you so much for the healing Mass and prayer card.' (Illinois)

It was the end of October, 1990 when Brigid Gormley finally accepted that her twin brother Owen was seriously ill. He'd been unwell for two years before that and a scan had shown up what the doctors called a cyst in the brain which, they said, was too small to operate on. The two years had passed in a mixture of apprehension and sometimes just disbelief. Surely nothing could happen to him, she had told herself on more than one occasion.

Yet, here he was in Belfast's Royal Hospital. Another scan had shown that the 'cyst' was much larger now. If they didn't operate, the doctors said, Owen would end up in a wheelchair at best.

They'd operated on Wednesday 5th December. The following Thursday the family were still waiting to confirm the results. When Owen was visited by his own doctor together with one of the leading specialists from Beaver Park, the city's cancer hospital, they didn't need to have the prognosis spelled out for them.

Owen would have to go to Beaver Park for further treatment, the doctors explained, before leaving him to examine the results of the latest tests and x-rays.

The next thirty minutes were the worst Owen had spent in his life. Over and over again in his mind he reconstructed the conversation with the specialists.

The growth was malignant and deep-rooted, they had told him. Had the operation been successful? It was difficult to say, they murmured, going back again to how deep-rooted the cyst had been. A programme of treatment would take place at Beaver Park. But they would give no assurances for the future.

Thirty minutes later they returned. Owen was unable to decipher the expression on their faces. They looked at him for some time. Owen found this unnerving. Obviously, the latest tests had shown an even more serious picture, he decided. Then they spoke.

There was no need for any further treatment, they said. At first he took this to mean that the situation was so desperate they weren't even attempting to combat it any further.

But no — they meant what they said — there was no need for any treatment.

What had happened to change their minds? They never explained that to Owen. In fact, when he questioned them they seemed at a loss for words.

After that, he never asked again for an explanation.

"There was no need," says Brigid, almost four years later.

"Owen has never looked back. Health-wise he is perfect. And we believe that a miracle took place. There is no other explanation."

But she does have an explanation as to how that miracle occurred.

"While Owen was very ill, a cousin of my mother's wrote a letter home to us and in with this she enclosed a little card. On one side was the picture of a priest, on the other something entitled the Miracle Prayer.

"I had never heard of Fr Peter Rookey before this, but reading that prayer for the first time it seemed like some sort of lifeline to me. I was so desperate that I would have tried anything, I suppose, but I started saying that prayer and every day after that I stormed heaven with it, asking for healing for my brother.

"I was so desperate in fact, that I felt it was really important that I did as it said at the end of the prayer, say it with feeling and belief. Sometimes, in an effort to achieve this, I would say it maybe ten times before I could convince myself that I had said it properly. And if I felt that my prayer was not good enough, did not come straight from the heart with total concentration, I would say it over again.

"Maybe that sounds strange, but you know the way it is when somebody you love is seriously ill. It's so difficult to keep your mind focused on anything, because it continually strays back to the ill person."

All through Owen's operation and throughout the following days, Brigid and the entire family continued to say the Miracle Prayer, a wealth of prayer pouring up from their homes in County Tyrone.

"And when she heard of the reversal of opinion and treatment for her twin brother, Brigid believed in her heart that Fr Peter Rookey's Miracle Prayer was powerfully responsible.

It was two years later in November 1993 when she first saw Fr Peter.

"He came to Northern Ireland and I went up to Fintanagh to see him," she recalls.

"Four or five of us in the family went together and after Mass when Father invited us for the blessing with oil, we went up also. Many people that night were experiencing what Fr Peter described as an experience with the Holy Spirit and one of our family felt this in a great way, resting in the spirit for some time."

She brought a letter with her to the healing Mass, telling Fr Peter of what had happened and thanking him for the prayer.

"I was too shy to go up and talk to him," she recalls, "but I put the letter into a box and wondered if he would ever get it. Two days later I had a reply.

"Never before had I experienced a miracle in my life, but I know this was one. And to this day I still say that prayer."

Chapter Eight

"STAND UP AND WALK!"

It's well after 11pm and despite the fact that Fr Peter has been up since before 6am that morning and travelling half the day, he still appears fresh and tireless. What's more, the sense of humour has not deserted him.

"What happens if we don't keep Jesus in our lives?" he asks.

I shake my head, expecting some deep spiritual revelation.

"We're like the duck flying upside down — we quack up!" Fr Peter laughs, the laughter increasing as he watches the bemused expression passing over my face. For a deeply spiritual man, he has a wide collection of jokes that only he could get away with, I tell him.

He's nonplused by my remark. Sometimes the jokes are shared before a healing Mass — 'to put the people at their ease,' he explains, a twinkle in his eye.

"The Lord has a sense of humour, I tell them," he continues. "He must have if He made us!"

The healing Mass that evening had been in a parish that Fr Rookey had not visited before, some four hours drive from Chicago. Relaxing over his first meal of the day, he chuckles as he remembers the silence that met his first jokes. It had taken the congregation several minutes to realise that the priest on the altar was full of the joy of the Lord, rather than anything else, and to warm to his personality.

And the evening had had its poignant moments, as when a woman had moved up to the microphone later and told how she had first gone to one of Fr Peter's healing Masses the previous year in another town, seeking healing for her husband who was diagnosed with terminal cancer.

They had both gone to the Mass more through desperation than faith, she confessed, both feeling bitter that at only forty-six her husband's expected lifespan had been reduced to a few months at best.

Father Peter had prayed with him she said and also with her. He had blessed them both with holy oil. Her husband had rested in the spirit, she had not, but had felt what seemed like a heatwave go through her body as Father had laid his hands on her husband standing beside her.

For many years, she went on to explain, neither she nor her husband had been near a church. Although brought up Catholics, of Italian extraction, they had both fallen well away from the faith.

Life had been good to them financially. They never had a family, but their own relationship was so close and so deep that the loss of a family was something they had been able to cope with together. And as far as their way of life went, well all she would say was that they were more than comfortable with a good savings deposit behind them.

When the cancer had been diagnosed they had sought every medical attention possible to achieve a healing. Nothing had worked and now they faced the pain of separation.

The healing Mass was the first church service they had attended for many years. They were both struck by the deep faith and obvious power of the priest as he prayed with others. They had watched people leave their wheelchairs and they had seen others, with tears pouring down their faces, walk away as if whatever they had come to seek healing for had been granted to them.

When it came their time to be blessed they approached the altar with confidence. A miracle would be worked and life would continue as it always had been. She was especially sure of this when she felt the heat run through her body and saw her husband fall back to be caught gently and left lying on the ground for several minutes.

And a miracle had taken place, she told the silent, listening congregation. Praise God, she added and they broke into applause.

When it died down she went on to explain the miracle.

It wasn't the physical healing they had expected, she continued quietly. Just one month later, her beloved husband had died in her arms. Jesus had not seen fit to heal him of his cancer, she explained, but a great spiritual healing had taken place in their lives. A peace, unlike any other they had ever experienced, had come into their hearts and lives that evening and had remained with them until death had parted them for a time on this earth. And that peace had continued for her until this day and would she knew, until some time in the future she was reunited with her husband in that promised world where God would wipe away the tears from all eyes.

The blessing they had received from Fr Peter, she finished, had achieved a healing that she could honestly say, given a choice, she would have to choose before the physical healing they had come seeking. They had both returned to the Church, to confession and Communion and the few short weeks they spent together were truly the happiest of their married lives.

She had come here tonight simply to thank Fr Rookey, she said.

Leaving the microphone she moved slowly towards Fr Peter who held out his arms to her. When she moved away to return to her seat, her face was wet with tears, but her expression one of peace. Wiping away the tears from my own face, I looked round in embarrassment to see whether anybody had noticed. All I could see were the tears on the faces of others all round me, as Fr Peter moved to the microphone and praised God for the healing that had been described so beautifully, a spiritual healing which, he reminded us, was worth so much more than renewed limbs.

And yet, I remind him, as we discuss the compelling witness of God's love that we'd heard that evening, examples of the blind seeing and the lame walking can have a tremendous effect on the faltering faith of others. I mean to say, I argue, it's difficult to dismiss the reality of God when you're brought face to face with an obvious physical miracle.

Heather Duncan's healing was one of these, I pointed out.

It was 1985 when the nerves at the base of her spine were irreparably damaged when, as a young nurse in Aberdeen, Scotland, she attempted to lift an elderly patient and fell.

The accident left her unable to walk and confined to a wheelchair. Three operations were attempted to reverse the damage. All three failed. Unable to work Heather, who was married with a young son, was eventually awarded a State Disability Allowance.

Attempting to come to terms with her disability, she took comfort from a book she read about the life of Padre Pio.

"By the time I'd finished this," she says, "I decided that I had been given a very special gift from God—the apostolate of suffering."

It was an attitude that made life more than bearable. The belief and practice of her faith became a very special part of her life.

"I never even asked why God had allowed this to happen to me. I felt that it was just an accident, but that somehow through it all God would find a way to use me in life."

Along with a group of friends she made preparations for a special trip to Medjugorje, Bosnia-Herzegovina, a pilgrimage of thanksgiving to God for the peace and joy that, despite her crippled limbs, filled her life.

Medjugorje was one of the most wonderful places she had ever visited, she recalls. A valley in which the presence of Jesus and Mary is tangible and where heaven seems to meet earth. Heather felt as though she was on the most special spiritual retreat of her life and spent many hours in and around the church, attending the Masses, devotions and Adoration, feeling spiritually renewed with each passing day.

When her friends told her about the healing service they were going to in the cemetery down behind the church, Heather wasn't interested.

"I refused to go," she says now.

"I knew that Jesus could heal me if He wished to do so, but I honestly believed this was not in His plan, otherwise the operations I had gone through would have been successful. I felt going to a healer was going against God's plan and told my friends that I intended to spend the morning in prayer at the foot of the big mountain with the cross on top.

"But they just wouldn't take no for an answer. I could go praying anywhere I wanted once I'd been to see this healing priest, they said. I remember being quite annoyed about it all, as they just spun my wheelchair around and took me down to join the crowds in the cemetery."

She insisted on remaining at the back of the crowd when they arrived, still not wishing to be there.

"I decided that I could pray the Rosary here as well as anywhere else, so I joined in with the crowd who were reciting it. I was sitting there with my head bowed and my eyes closed when it suddenly struck me that we'd said a lot more than the ten Hail Mary's that make up a decade of the Rosary. So I looked up to see what on earth was going on.

"The people were standing there with their hands held up, as if they were praying over somebody, then a couple of minutes later the crowd parted and a girl came through, pushing her wheelchair. She was crying and I just knew that she had been healed. I sat there and thanked God for bringing out this miracle for her."

As the praying continued, Heather joined in again before being interrupted by her friends who had seen the miraculous cure.

"They wanted to bring me up to the priest, but I refused. Again I told them that I just didn't believe that God wanted to heal me. And I really felt that my life was as it was meant to be."

Against her will, she says, her friends ignored her arguments and began to push her through the crowd which moved back to allow the wheelchair through.

A short time later, Fr Rookey stopped in front of her and asked what her problem was.

Did she have any chance of improvement?

No, she told him.

The priest then gave her his crucifix to hold and told her to look at Jesus. She did so and for the next fifteen minutes, she says, all she was aware of was Jesus on the cross and an intense heat in her body. All round her the people continued to pray the Rosary, but Heather was not aware of this.

"Then I felt something tugging at the crucifix. I knew that somebody wanted to take Jesus away from me, but I did not want to let Him go, and held tightly on to it. I heard the Hail Mary being said then, and I realised that my prayers were necessary for the healing of somebody, so I joined in.

"Moments later, I realised that it was Fr Peter who was trying to take the crucifix out of my hands. I struggled inside myself, decided whether or not I should let it go. All I wanted was to hold on to Jesus. Then it occurred to me that I had to give it back to him, so that he could heal others around me and I let it go."

She remembers Fr Peter asking her, then, if she believed that Jesus could heal her.

The answer to that question was simple, Heather says. Of course she knew that Jesus could heal her if He wished. But she didn't believe that this was His intention.

"Fr Rookey asked me did I want to take a step in faith, I looked at him and I told him yes, I did.

"I'll never forget the words he said to me next. It was like something from a biblical scene.

"Silver and gold have I not," he said, "but what I have I give you.

"In the name of Jesus, stand up and walk."

And she did.

As those around her gasped, Heather stood up and stepped away from her wheelchair.

"I could stand up straight and I had no pain whatsoever," she says, the entire wonderful happening imprinted forever on her mind.

"It was the first time since the accident that I had been without pain. It was miraculous. I just walked away from the chair and my legs felt strong and normal. As a nurse, I knew that the years should have left my legs weak, the muscles wasted, but it was as if the accident had never happened."

The remainder of the week passed in a blaze of happiness. She felt like singing. Her life had been returned to her unblemished. And she felt full of love and gratitude towards the priest whose prayers had brought God's healing into her damaged body.

Home again, she went for medical tests.

The doctors were astounded. New x-rays showed that the spine was still crushed and damaged, she was told. Walking was a medical impossibility. Compared with the x-rays that had been taken when she was told she would never walk again, there was no difference.

And yet, she was walking — and running, up and down stairs, carrying weights, defying medical science.

Before going to Medjugorje, her life had been restricted to the third floor apartment in a block of flats. The only time she left home was when the ambulance men carried her down to go to the hospital. Now, the world opened up to her.

Heather believes she received two miraculous cures in her life. The first was when, confined to a wheelchair, she had time to think about the faith that she no longer practised.

Over those years of pain, she had come to know Jesus, she says, as her loving Saviour. Despite the months and months of pain and suffering, she never lost that faith, accepting the suffering as a blessing for somebody else, some unknown person who needed it.

The second miracle was when Fr Peter Rookey laid his hands on her and called on the power of Christ to heal her body, as He had undoubtedly healed her soul.

Chapter Nine

A NEW JOY

'Dear Fr Rookey,

I was here in Florida to see my own doctor regarding surgery. I have been living in upstate New York for the last four months, taking care of a terminally ill aunt. Two doctors and a radiologist in New York diagnosed me with ovarian cancer and scheduled surgery for me. Now I know God had other plans for me — in meeting you.

My husband and I came to your healing Mass two times and I rested in the spirit both times.

Father, on Sunday when I arrived in front of the church I smelled beautiful tea roses all round the car and as I walked to the front of the church. It was such an experience. The heat rushed through me during those four hours of praying — amazing! I kept saying to my husband, 'Why is it so hot in here?'

Resting in the spirit was the most wonderful feeling. I'll never forget it. Praise the Lord!!

After those two experiences at the healing Masses, I had my doctor's appointment and exams rescheduled. All tests have come back normal. I no longer need surgery. Praise Jesus!' (New York)

It's early morning and the mist that has hung over the Dublin mountains is beginning to lift. The road we are taking into the city leads us past fields where sheep graze and lambs play. A cow looks over a fence taking only lazy interest in our passing, more concerned with the calf that suckles by her side. After two days of rain Ireland is at her greenest, the summer sun already drying the pools and sparkling against the sides of white-washed farmhouses.

We climb higher, up and over the mountains, past pine forests and across rocky hillsides until finally we turn a bend in the road and there, spread out before us, is the city of Dublin nestling beside the bay with the Irish sea at its back.

The wind blows through the open window on Fr Peter's side of the car and I'm instantly reminded of the breath of God in our lives, the Holy Spirit that travels with us everywhere waiting for the invitation to come into our souls and blow away the trappings of worldly longings.

At the healing Mass the previous day I had been surprised by the large number of people who, when blessed by Fr Peter, had immediately rested in the spirit, some for ten or fifteen minutes. Most noticeable of all had been the children who had gone down like so many tiny skittles and were later helped to their feet looking just as if they had slept for hours and the sleep had not yet left their eyes.

I remembered too, the disappointment of one woman who remained standing, while all others around her fell back into waiting arms.

Some people who don't rest in the spirit after being blessed, I remark to Fr Peter, feel that they haven't experienced a healing. That the healing will only come if they fall.

"It's a question I'm often asked," Fr Peter replies, winding the window down still further.

"Why did that person rest in the spirit and I did not? I must be less holy than she is, so God is not prepared to heal me.

"Well, it's not like that at all, you see. The Spirit breathes where He will. It would be like my asking God why did you give that one the gift of prophecy and I don't have it? Or why give this one the gift of tongues, but not me? All of these are the gifts of the Holy Spirit, and we must accept whatever the Spirit gives and be happy with that.

"But people get so caught up with this, that we printed a little flyer explaining it all and any time I have a healing Mass, if it's the first time at such a Mass for most of the congregation, I take time to explain what happens when people rest in the spirit.

"I tell them it's a beautiful rendezvous with the Lord, but if they don't experience it that doesn't mean that God has passed them by. Some people don't fall down, they rest standing up. And some experience a feeling of peace wash over them, but they too remain on their feet. Those who do rest in the spirit however, generally experience a tremendous sensation of peace and very often during this time the healing takes place. Especially inner healing, which is even more important than physical healing.

"But it's not necessary to rest in the spirit to be healed."

Some experience this meeting with the Lord on their very first visit to a healing Mass, he continues, while others attend healing services a number of times before all of a sudden resting in the spirit.

"So, if you don't rest tonight, be patient, because you may well do so another time. And keep attending healing Masses, because you can never have enough healing in your lives, just as nobody has ever died of too many hugs!"

While not resting in the spirit is no block to healing, he adds, unforgiveness certainly is.

"Sometimes we need to look into our souls and see are we blocking our own healing. For example, is there anybody of whom we should be asking forgiveness? Or perhaps we have not forgiven ourselves for some happening, so are not able to receive the love of God. Because if I can't love myself, then I can't love my neighbour, nor can I love God. There's a contradiction there inside myself.

"What we need to do, if we are seeking healing, is to leave our gifts at the altar, then go seeking reconciliation with God and with those around us. After this we are in a position to come back and make our requests and receive the gift of God's healing."

We reach the security barrier into Radio Telefis Eireann, Ireland's national radio and television station. Within ten minutes Fr Peter is on the airwaves on one of the leading morning radio programmes. The interview had been scheduled for six or seven minutes, but as the presenter takes Fr Peter through his beliefs and an account of the healing ministry to which God has called him, those six minutes stretch to forty.

The effect on a listening nation is unbelievable. Within minutes of Fr Peter's leaving the studio, the switchboard lights up to what the presenter — discussing the event on air next morning — calls 'near meltdown'. The office is unable to handle the number of calls flooding in. For the next three days the radio programme follows Fr Peter's progress through Ireland, doing live reports from some of the healing Masses, interviewing people who claim to having been healed through his prayers and discussing what they call 'the phenomenon of this extraordinary man' with clergy and lay people alike.

Every Mass Fr Peter holds is attended by thousands. In some places the venues have to be changed to larger churches to try to accommodate the people who flock to them, but even this is not enough. Church doors are closed and thousands wait patiently outside for their opportunity to go in and receive the priest's blessing as those inside finally leave. It's well after midnight each night when Fr Peter blesses the last person seeking healing.

When he turns to give me a hug and blessing in the sacristy after one four-hour session, I realise that his clothes are wet with perspiration.

We take up the discussion of resting in the spirit some days later.

One of the most beautiful accounts he has ever read of this experience, he says, was written by a fellow Servite, Fr Tim Flynn , now Provincial of the Servants of Mary in Ireland.

Fr Tim's experience occurred at a time when the Servite Order in Ireland was disturbed by the media coverage given to Fr Rookey's two-weekly visits to Ireland each year, and unsure as to whether they wished to allow him to continue practising the ministry in Ireland. The chief reason for this was the huge publicity that was given to the thousands of people who were reported to rest in the spirit.

Reading the account Fr Tim Flynn later sent of his experience, I was struck by the obvious working of the Holy Spirit in the situation. Not long after it had occurred, Fr Flynn was made Provincial of the Order. If it hadn't been for his own experience of resting in the spirit, would he have remained open to Fr Peter's continued visits to Ireland?

The following is his own report:

'In this reflection I would like to share my own experience of being 'slain in the Spirit,' or of 'resting in the Spirit' as it is more commonly called. It is very much a personal experiential description. My experience occurred during the recent visit of Fr Peter Mary Rookey to Ireland.

I suppose I could describe myself as an unlikely candidate for this experience. I had heard of this phenomenon, had spoken about it with some experienced leaders in the Charismatic Renewal, especially with Larry Kelly of Belfast and I was aware of the book by Cardinal Suenens called *'Resting in the Spirit'* though I had never seriously read it. I believed in the experience, but mostly for other people.

As with the gift of tongues that my evangelical friend prayed so long and so hard that I would receive at the beginnings of the Charismatic Renewal in the early seventies, I never really received these gifts. I concluded that I was far too proper and inhibited to allow myself to be a 'fool' even for Christ's sake. Furthermore, I would probably now describe myself as a 'fallen away' charismatic. Though very appreciative of its value, my only contact is by accepting invitations to celebrate the Eucharist for different groups, mainly in the Dublin area.

From my earliest days in religious life, my main prayer for spiritual gifts was that I would grow more deeply to love God with all my being and the brother and sister as Christ would want me to love them. In a word, my spiritual desire was to love with the Heart of Christ. All spiritual gifts or 'touches of grace' in my life were seen in relation to this over-riding desire. That is why the experience 'slain in the Spirit' was such a surprise to me.

Fr Rookey came to Ireland as he has done in recent years for a series of Healing Services throughout Ireland. I invited him to celebrate the Eucharist at the Servite Oratory/St Peregrine Centre at the Rathfarnham Shopping Centre and to conduct a Healing Service on the day of his arrival. I have known Peter since I was a young religious at Benburb thirty or more years ago. I also knew that the Lord used him as an instrument of healing when he was in Benburb in the early 1950's.

Like many others in the healing ministry, there are divided opinions as to Fr Peter's approach. Yet I was convinced that there was something very valuable in his ministry and wanted to give those who came to the Oratory a chance to experience it. Nevertheless, I was very anxious about what would happen. What would people think? Would they understand what was happening? Would it upset them? What would my own Superiors or other friars think or say? What would happen if there were complaints to the Archbishop's House? As Director of the Servite Ministry at the Oratory I felt responsible and one of my biggest fears concerned the 'resting in the Spirit'.

At the end of the Mass when Peter began his ministry, having reminded the people that God's healing love can and does touch the woundedness of the whole person, body, mind and spirit, he emphasised in his 'one-liner': 'Hate and be sick, love and be well, at peace. There were plenty of people 'resting in the Spirit,' so that by the end of the service it was part of the 'happening'.

It was then that Heather Duncan, who was cured of a serious back complaint which had her crippled and in a wheelchair, invited me to be blessed.

Fully protected in my Servite Habit, I stood in front of Fr Peter. I can remember thinking 'I will not fall'. Fr Peter blessed me with the Blessed Oil and the Crucifix containing the relics of Servite Saints and Blesseds. Out I went.

I would like to describe my experience in two phases:

i) what exactly happened and ii) what I perceive as the effects of this experience. I am well aware that my description is very inadequate and falls well short of capturing the real sense of this wonderful 'touch of the Spirit' in my life.

I was deeply conscious of the presence of God. I experienced a deep sense of peace and relaxation. It was as if all the tensions of the years drained out of my body. I was at peace in body, in mind and in spirit. It was a most profound resting. I could scarcely lift my arms so relaxed was I.

This experience must have lasted for at least a half an hour. At one point I remember thinking I will never get up again, and it didn't really matter. I was also aware of what was going on around me though it seemed very much in the distance. The people present were praying the Chaplet of Divine Mercy, which I hadn't heard prayed aloud before. As I heard the words: 'For the sake of His sorrowful Passion, have mercy on us and on the whole world' repeated over and over again, it seemed like I was being bathed in waves of warm refreshing water.

I can also remember praying for individual people who were suffering a lot and who had come to the Oratory to ask us to pray for them. I was also conscious of allowing hurts from the past, especially those around my years as Master of Students and Prior, to be taken away. I felt that I wanted to weep during those moments. I was also conscious of wanting to be fully available to God's plan for me. What mattered most was that I do His will. This brought great peace as I had been thinking about the future direction of my life in terms of ministry and service to the Order/Church. 'In His will is our peace.'

As I suffer with my stomach when under stress or when I'm over-tired, and the anxiety around Fr Peter's visit didn't help, I was conscious of my stomach muscles being relaxed as if healing had taken place. I prayed that this be so. There were also moments when I thought I was holding everyone back. It was already well past closing time at the Shopping Centre. Yet I couldn't really move, so profound was the sense of peace and relaxation. Underneath it all was the sense of God's presence, of His nearness and my only response could be to remain motionless. When I finally got up I had to be helped to sit on a chair. It was like being in the world, but not of it.

What are the effects of this experience?

Firstly, all the anxieties about Fr Peter's visit/ministry evaporated. There was a profound sense of God's presence. I wanted to pray all the time. I was profoundly touched by the sheer beauty, goodness and attractiveness of God. So much that the next day when I had to go into town and I purchased the paper to read on the bus on the way home, my desire to pray was so strong that I couldn't concentrate on reading and prayed instead.

I went from being physically and psychologically tired to having a new energy. A joy in life had returned.

My step was certainly lighter.

Gone were the feelings of self-pity — Why was I the only priest left in the Priory for most of the summer? As long as I was doing God's will it didn't matter any more. Comparing myself with other friars was now irrelevant. I found myself waking at night and praying, especially the psalms. I felt called to pray the 'Miracle Prayer' (composed by Fr Peter) many times daily. I began to pray the Chaplet of Divine Mercy.

And of course, I was terribly amused at what happened to me and found myself smiling that I, who see myself as always too dignified in public, should be stretched out in front of the Altar complete with my habit and with so many of the people I serve looking on. I wondered if this was the only way God could get through to me. And of course I was profoundly touched at God's goodness and graciousness to me. 'The mercies of the Lord I shall sing forever'.

There was a sense that 'I can do all things with the help of Him who strengthens me.' I was also aware of a new sense of joy in the Lord's service. And above all, the consciousness of God's immense love for me and for all the world and the desire to respond to it was overwhelming.

With babbling words more characteristic of a child, I have tried to describe an indescribable experience. I am very conscious that this experience of the Spirit is sheer gift, unmerited, undeserved— God's graciousness breaking into my life unexpectedly and almost unwelcome.

My prayer is as it has been over the years, that the experience will help me to love with the Heart of Christ.

'Resting in the Spirit' seems the right description for what happened that July evening.

Tim M. Flynn, OSM, August 13th, 1991.'

Chapter Ten

NO LONGER SILENT

It was almost six o'clock in the evening when Peggy Campbell remembered the healing service her friends had invited her to attend. Did she really want to go? She had told Cissie Maguire that basically she wasn't interested. And yet, here she was, looking at her watch and wondering whether or not to pick up the telephone. Cissie was the one who organised the local pilgrimage to Lourdes each year. Peggy had gone along with her on that, travelling to the Marian shrine in the hope that she would get relief from the back trouble that had been plaguing her. The visit to Lourdes had been beautiful, inspiring, but it had made no difference to the pain in her back. And she would have been happy to have been relieved of that pain simply because it made her working life so difficult at times. As a nurse in the Mid-Ulster hospital, she needed to be in the whole of her health when it came to dealing with patients.

Again she looked at the telephone. It was 6pm. If she was going to telephone Cissie she had better do it now. Picking up the telephone, she dialled the number that linked her from her own home in Cookstown to Cissie's place in Magherafelt.

"Cissie, it's Peggy," she whispered when the telephone was answered.

"Are you going to this healing service you've been talking about?"

Cissie had forgotten all about it, she discovered. Peggy was sorry that she had reminded her. She would have preferred to spend the evening at home. Too late now, she sighed as she replaced the telephone receiver. Cissie, reminded of the event, was determined not to miss it and equally determined to bring Peggy with her. Herself and Martin Devlin would take care of Peggy, she promised. And the back was so bad at the moment, that she may as well travel in her wheelchair. With the crush that was expected in the Football Club pavilion in Swatragh, Peggy could find herself in trouble if she tried to walk or stand for a long time.

There was barely time to get herself ready before Cissie and Martin arrived.

As usual, Peggy found it impossible to converse properly in the car, the sound of the engine drowning the soft whisper in which she talked.

She had never been totally at ease in a car since her accident a few years back. It had been a bad accident, but thank God she had recovered from it, apart from this back trouble. Then, strangely and without warning, over a year after the accident had occurred, she awoke one morning to find that she had lost her voice.

At first she'd put it down to laryngitis. As time went by and her voice didn't return beyond a small forced whisper, she began to fear cancer. An uncle of hers had lost his voice in the past. Eventually they discovered that he had cancer. She spent nights awake, facing the same possibility.

Eventually picking up the courage to go to her doctor, he sent her to hospital for tests. She was assured that no cancer had been found. The medical people had no explanation for the loss of her voice to the low whisper. With cancer ruled out however, Peggy felt she could cope with the difficulty.

"Looking back now," she recalls, "I don't know how I did it. I never missed a day from work, but it was very difficult to nurse patients and only be able to talk to them in a whisper.

"I was a little annoyed at the doctors also, who put my voice loss down to a reaction to the car accident. It was the only thing they could come up with, but to me it seemed a ridiculous suggestion. If I was going to have a psychological reaction to the accident, why did I not have it straight away, rather than a full year later? Besides, I was the last person who could be accused of suffering from any nervous disorder. Right through the two and a half years that my voice was restricted to a whisper, I never lost a day from work."

It had been a very frustrating couple of years, she admitted. When she went out to a social event with her husband people would talk to him, not to her. 'Has she got her voice back yet?' they would enquire, as if she was also deaf. And when it came to discussions she could never get her point across, because few people were willing to remain quiet enough to allow her whispering to be heard.

Most frustrating of all was when she would talk to people and they would answer yes, or no — in all the wrong places. It was obvious that they hadn't been able to hear what she said, but pretended to do so.

As Cissie and Martin drove her to the healing service, however, her voice problems were the last thing in her mind.

"If they had said to me that I should attend the service because it might help to bring back my voice, I wouldn't have gone near it," she says.

"I had tried everything possible to help restore my voice and nothing had worked. I had been to doctors, to speech therapy for two years and I'd even been to faith healers. And nothing worked.

"But I was hoping that maybe the healing service would do something to improve my back problem, which was bothering me so much at the time."

This July Thursday evening, it seemed as if the whole of Ulster had decided to travel to Swatragh. Cissie and Martin pushed Peggy's wheelchair through the crowds and Peggy thought how cold the midsummer evening was. Queuing outside the club building, Peggy shivered several times as the wind blew around her.

Inside however, the hall was hot and almost airless, so many people packed in to a confined space. Because she was in a wheelchair, Cissie and Martin were invited to bring her up the front where several other wheelchairs were already placed.

"If I hadn't been in the chair and up at the front, I would never have waited to be prayed with," Peggy recalls firmly.

"As Fr Rookey began to bless the sick, people fell back on the ground. That scared me. I just couldn't understand what was meant to be going on.

"But before I had time to flee, Fr Rookey was standing in front of me, asking about my problem. I started to tell him about my back, but of course the words only came out in a whisper. I don't know whether or not he heard what I was saying, but he obviously decided that my voice — or lack of it — was the problem. He blessed me, put the crucifix he carried to my lips and asked me to say 'Jesus'. I tried, and of course the word came out in a whisper.

"He spoke to me again. 'Say JESUS' he said in a loud voice — and I did! I said 'Jesus' and the name came out loud and strong. I actually didn't think for a moment that it was me speaking. I remember thinking: 'That noise couldn't be coming out of me'. It had been so long since I had heard my own voice and it sounded just awful, I thought."

As Fr Peter moved on, Peggy turned to her friends, so excited that she couldn't stop talking. Cissie and Martin were overjoyed for her. As soon as they could get her through the crowds they took her to a telephone which was out of bounds except to club members, but which was made available to Peggy when the officials were told the story.

Her hands shaking, she dialled her own home number. Her husband answered.

"It's me... Peggy," she babbled. "I've been healed, the priest blessed me at the healing service and my voice has returned..."

For a moment there was silence, then her husband's voice came angrily down the line.

"I don't know who you are, or why you are doing this," he said. "But let me tell you that I don't find it one bit funny..."

"He just didn't believe it was me!" Peggy laughs today, almost three years after her wonderful experience.

"Cissie had to take the telephone and call him back and assure him that it had been me on the phone. When I went home that night we just talked and talked for hours. Now that I had my voice back, I just couldn't stop talking."

When Peggy eventually went to bed that night, she was exhausted, talked out, but over the next couple of days such was her excitement that every waking moment seemed to be spent talking.

"Then, on Saturday night, at 8pm my voice went again," she recalls.

"I just couldn't believe it. It nearly broke my heart. I cried and cried and I remember thinking, surely God wouldn't be so cruel as to give me back my voice and then take it away again?

"I was crying when I telephoned John Gunning, the man who had arranged Fr Rookey's visit to Swatragh. I told him what had happened and he promised to see what he could do."

It took John Gunning a couple of days to catch up with Fr Peter who was criss-crossing Ireland, sometimes saying two healing Masses a day. Eventually he managed to talk to him and explain what had happened to Peggy.

"It was Saturday when my voice went again, and Monday evening before Fr Peter made contact with me. I think I had spent the last two days crying, but he was so reassuring to me. He told me that I had to remember that my voice had been away for two and a half years, so it was out of practice so to speak and may come and go for a time. But he said not to panic, it would come back.

"And he told me he believed that I had been healed."

As Fr Peter spoke to Peggy over the telephone, a strange thing happened, she says.

"When Cissie and Martin had helped me up out of my chair the previous Thursday so that Fr Rookey could bless me, they both told me later that as the priest prayed with me they felt what they described as an awful warmth spread right through their bodies. I felt nothing.

"Yet, as Fr Rookey now talked to me on the phone and told me he believed that I had been healed, I suddenly felt the most intense heat go right through my body, from the top of my head right down to my big toe. It scared the life out of me."

A short time later, at exactly 8pm she remembers clearly, Peggy's voice returned — and has never left her since.

"If anybody had told me that such a thing could happen," she says, "I would have been very cynical. Yet, it did happen and I believe that it was miraculous.

"How could it be described as anything else? Right through those years, as I worked away, thousands of people knew that I could only talk in a whisper. Now it's clear that I am healed. I remember the first time I met an ex-patient who had been in the hospital for three months and right through that time had never heard me talking. When we bumped into each other again and I said 'hello' I'll never forget the amazed look on his face. 'You've got your voice back!' he said — and I told him how. In fact, any time that anybody has asked how I suddenly began to speak again, I have told them how it happened.

"And I've told them that when Cissie and Martin were taking me to the healing service and I said in a moment of irritation that I had no faith in all this, they replied, 'We have enough faith for you.' And so they had."

The total humility and acceptance of the priest who healed her, in the face of such an obviously miraculous event, is something that has remained strongly with Peggy.

"After Fr Rookey prayed over me and I suddenly spoke, he simply moved on to the next person. I suppose I expected him to make a big event of the healing, but no! I didn't even have time to thank him, before he had moved away.

"To him, who constantly sees God working miracles, it was as if nothing strange had happened.

"To me it was everything."

Chapter Eleven

'BELIEVE MY WORKS'

'Dear Fr Rookey,

I am writing this letter to tell you about some exciting news and to thank you for your continued prayers and support.

Two years ago at Easter we came over to meet you and listen to you and pray with you. My mother was suffering with a non-curable kidney disease with a very long name, which caused deterioration of the kidneys. That evening you prayed over all of us and you spoke to my mother for a long time.

I later wrote to you and asked for your continued prayers. My mother continued to pray to Our Lord and His Holy Mother very intensely. My family and friends and relatives also continued to pray for her recovery.

We all continued our prayers. Then a few months later her daily blood test started to read on the low side. The doctor reduced her intake of insulin. The low readings continued until she stopped the injections completely. Her doctor doesn't understand this complete turnaround in her condition. He told her to continue to do whatever it is that she's doing, because she looks and feels terrific.

She now has no signs of diabetes and her kidneys have stopped deteriorating. Her medication for water retention swelling have been reduced to next to nothing. She now goes out again and has returned to praying in Church. She is totally convinced that the Lord has heard all of our prayers and is responsible for her recovery. We are too! Praise the Lord!!' (Massachusetts)

"I do not cause healings to happen," Fr Peter says firmly. "Jesus is the healer. I am only His instrument and He does the curing while I lay on my hands, pray over the person, encourage faith and acceptance.

"The power to heal rests only in the hands of God the Son, born of the Virgin Mary in Bethlehem over two thousand years ago. During his public ministry Jesus healed the sick, the lame, even public sinners. And He told His disciples to continue this ministry after He returned to His Father.

"And so they did and the power He sent them turned them from being terrified cowering men hidden in the Upper Room, to the strong brave men who went out to preach the Gospel.

"He left those gifts to us, at Pentecost, but sometimes we're too unsure to take them up.

"And yet, we should take up His ministry with confidence, because it was our Blessed Lord Himself who gave it to us. In His last address to His apostles, before He left to sit at the right hand of the Father, He told them that those who believed these signs He had given, would follow in His name.

"In My name they will speak strange tongues, they will cast out demons. They will be able to take up scorpions and perchance they should drink polluted water they will not be harmed. The sick on whom they lay their hands will recover."

"Those were His words.

"And then, if we think back to the last lines of St James' epistle, which are used by every priest when dispensing the Sacrament of the Sick, the lines written by the saint who was the cousin of Our Lord, he tells us: 'If anyone is sick among you, let them bring in the elders of the church and they will lay their hands upon them and anoint them with oil and they shall recover, and if they be in sin then their sins will be forgiven them.'

"Well, all of these words and many more in the New Testament point to the mandate given to us by the Lord, to lay hands on the sick. When He sent out the apostles to evangelise, as we discussed earlier, He said: 'Go into the towns and villages and announce the kingdom of God is at hand, reform your lives.'

"Heal the sick, He told them and of course He performed many miracles of healing to back up His words and strengthen the faith of the people.'If you don't believe My words, believe My works,' He said."

Yet, despite this mandate to heal, much of the Church hierarchy has looked with apprehension and little favour on such ministries as the one Fr Peter practices.

The crowds who flocked to the Benburb Priory seeking healing in such huge numbers disturbed the Servite superiors. While not disputing that healings were taking place, they felt that the resultant publicity could be damaging to the ordinary faith of people.

After six years, Fr Peter was transferred from Northern Ireland to Rome in 1954 and appointed to an administrative position as Consulator to the Father General of the Order of the Servants of Mary.

He was also asked to cease his healing services.

The move was not a demotion, they pointed out, but more an opportunity for the Order to take stock of the apparent gift that God had bestowed on the young priest, and to give Fr Peter the opportunity to use his other talents in the service of the Lord.

The gift, if it was truly such, would stand the test of time.

Fr Peter felt no resentment towards the move, accepting the pain of 'silencing' with the same humility and resignation that Padre Pio had adopted to his superiors.

"I have often said to the Lord, 'It's Your will where our fulfilment lies — in doing Your will.'

"Padre Pio was suspended from doing the work to which he believed God had called him, for fifteen years. And I remember, when I spoke to Padre Pio and asked his advice on an important matter at one time, that advice was to do everything under obedience."

One of his favourite reminders to himself, he says, when he has been faced with painful opposition to his ministry, has been the thought from the book of Proverbs — 'The obedient man will speak of his victory'.

"When I left Ireland early in 1954, I had been working considerably in the healing ministry. But once I left I had every other kind of job but healing," he recalls.

He spent six years in Rome holding down the Office of Assistant General of the Servite Order in the city, followed by three years ministering in the International College in Lausanne where his degrees from Loyola and DePaul Universities in Chicago stood him in good stead. After that came five years in Germany followed by service in Sweden, the Middle East and even a sixteen year stint on the missions in the Ozarks — over two hundred miles of territory to cover in ministering to the Servite churches there. Along the way he learned to speak seven languages.

"Finally, a Provincial whom I'd had as a student in Rome so many years before, a beautiful man, brought me back to Chicago to begin this work of healing again in the Basilica where I was ordained.

"So that's where it all began again. And if the Lord will forgive me comparing myself with Him, I consider those years like the thirty years He spent behind the carpenter's lathe. Why wasn't He out there as we say in colloquial language, 'socking it to them' for years beforehand, preaching the gospel, healing people and so on? God's ways are not our ways and now, with all that experience behind me, I feel that He is working more powerfully through me than perhaps He might have done if I had just continued in this ministry all along."

One of the great joys of Fr Peter's life is that he now has the full support of his Order behind him in the ministry he undertakes with such love.

The letter of recommendation he shows me has been long-awaited perhaps, but its arrival was sweet.

To Whom It May Concern:

Father Peter M. Rookey, OSM is a solemn professed friar of the Order of Servants of Mary and a member of the Eastern Province of Servites in the United States.

As his major superior and personal Ordinary, I certify that he is a priest in good standing with faculties to preach and hear confessions which may be exercised in accord with the norm of law.

Father Rookey's ministry of preaching, healing and compassion has brought solace to many and contributes to the spiritual building of the Church. He has my permission to pursue this ministry, without prejudice to the rights of the local Ordinary.

Given at Our Lady of Sorrows Monastery, Chicago on this date of 13th September, 1991

Very Rev, John M. Huels, OSM
Prior Provincial

Along with his designation by Pope John Paul II as a Knight of the Holy Sepulchre (and the photograph showing His Holiness honouring him with this) the letter above is one of the very few personal possessions that Fr Peter has. Add to this one very worn black Servite habit, one white lightweight habit for visiting hot climates, a well-worn pair of sandals and an even more worn pair of shoes and you have Fr Peter's sole worldly possessions. Those and the black bag he carries everywhere with him containing his breviary, prayer books and phials of holy oil, letters to which he must reply, some prayer cards, a couple of pairs of Rosary beads given to him in the Holy Land (which he immediately proceeds to give as gifts) and a spare set of underwear.

Compared with the possessions that most of us gather along the way, it's a humble collection and has taken him since his birthdate on October 12th, 1916 to accumulate.

And yet, I wonder, watching him as he waves goodbye at the airport, which of us is the richer?

Chapter Twelve

SO MUCH BEAUTY

'Dear Fr Rookey,

Maybe you will be surprised to receive a letter from the Netherlands.

Time flies quickly. In May 1991, I was in Medjugorje for the seventh time. There I met a Belgium religious. Her family told me about your help in Medjugorje. It was just the last day before I left.

It was a great mercy for me to receive your salvation and help. The Holy Spirit sent me to you, Father. I had a tumour in my small intestine, also behind my ear. I was so very happy to meet you. I didn't understand all that you said as you spoke too fast, but inside I was understanding.

The Spirit of power came over me. After this I met you again for a short conversation. You laid your arm around me to embrace the Holy Cross.

The Gospa asks us always to pray, pray, pray in her messages. Somebody gave me a little print from you. I say this prayer every day. In my mind I see your Holy Cross and feel the Holy Spirit. I saw a girl walking again and a little boy who has light again in his eyes. There were very great miraculous signs. I was so happy to see it. I'll never forget that you did this holy work in the name of the Holy Spirit.

Dear Father Rookey, I wish you more and more the Holy Salvation and Power for all the people.'

(Leeuwarden, Holland.)

It was evening when Sylvia felt inspired to sit down and chronicle the many happenings she had witnessed since first meeting Fr Peter Rookey. The list took the Asian-American woman some time, stretching as it did from the United States to Europe and even the Philippines.

When she had finished, she sat back in the quietness of her Houston, Texas home and read over it, seeming to relive each event as it happened.

Medjugorje, Republic of Bosnia and Herzegovina: June 1991...

The Renewal of Holy Order Vows for priests at the main altar of the Franciscan Monastery Church of Siroki Brijeg deeply touched me. The Holy Spirit pervaded the entire congregation. The ceremony was officiated by Fr Jozo Zovko, OFM and Fr Peter Rookey, OSM.

My immediate response was to thank God for all the good priests in the world and in the same breath, forgive all the bad priests in my life.

I begged Our Lady Queen of Peace to allow me to work with the priest of Her choice, in thanksgiving for all the blessings given to me and my family. The next day at the back of St James Church, under a huge green tent, while Fr Peter and other priests were helping pilgrims, I assisted many persons who were slain in the spirit to get back on their feet. I also sought to comfort those moved to tears.

Houston, Texas: November 1992...

Many children came forward with pictures of their guardian angels and patron saints. Fr Peter was almost overwhelmed by the clamour of the emotionally disturbed, retired nuns and severely handicapped Vietnamese refugees.

He prayed fifteen decades of the Rosary for one Muslim woman while she enjoyed her first encounter with the Holy Spirit. Revived, she voiced her desire to become a convert. Fr Peter advised her husband to present her to their parish priest.

Washington DC: March 1993...

Terminally ill patients went to the Healing Masses and Reconciliation Services at the Basilica of the National Shrine of the Immaculate Conception.

A homeless Irishman who had faithfully followed Fr Peter in his healing services, promised to evangelise other street persons so that they would return to the Church.

Fresno, California: September 1993...

Several family unifications took place during the healing Masses. Persons severely damaged by occult belief and drug addiction resolved to amend their lives.

A Los Angeles assistant of Bishop Arzube shared his crucifix which contained relics of Padre Pio. An inspired lady wrote a poem to honour Fr Peter's healing touch.

Sacramento, California: September 1993...

Pilgrims from Ireland, Mexico, Philippines, Los Angeles and Nevada (among them Fr Peter's own blood brother,

Tom) give testimony to diverse types of healing received in the past forty five years from Fr Peter.

A single mother was reunited with her emotionally disturbed daughter. Many reported seeing the presence of their dearly departed loved ones at all the healing Masses.

Luzon, Visayas and Mindanao, Philippines: October 1993...

Continuous prayer yielded instantaneous miracles ranging from inner conversions to physical healing and happy deaths.

Many priests, consecrated nuns, lay ministers, childless couples, individuals, families, prisoners, drug addicts, unwed mothers, street urchins and ICU patients attested to their personal encounter with the Lord.

Hordes of poor families walked miles carrying their sick to the Cathedrals and churches on iron chairs and sleeping mats.

Several TV, radio and newspaper reports touched the lives of persons unable to attend Fr Peter's services.

The holiness, prayerfulness and individualised concern given by Fr Peter to every man, woman and child had untold influence on the spirituality of their faith.

Tears of joy freely flowed from both Fr Peter and us Filipinos — recipients of his love and devotion to the Blessed Sacrament, God the Holy Spirit, and Our Lady of Sorrows.

The scenes she had witnessed returned vividly to her mind, but it was more than that, she suddenly realised.

The pictures that had flowed through her mind were one thing — the lessons learned from the experiences were something else. Something even more important.

Reaching for her pen once again, Sylvia added to what she had already written:

1. Lessons taught throughout Fr Rookey's Healing Missions;

a. The presence of Divine Intervention — the reality and truth promulgated in the Gospels are re-enacted throughout the Servite Rosary, the Holy Mass, the Exposition of the Blessed Sacrament and the Healing services.

b. Changes necessary to improve a person's spirituality; God oriented and total participation in all religious services leads to a way of life that is conducive to love of God, self and neighbour.

2. Lessons learned by the faithful recipient; Sanctity of death, the anointing of ICU patients and the kissing of their feet in preparation for a joyful encounter with our loving Father and Creator.

3. Planting of seeds for inner conversion;

a. Seeds of courage
b. Seeds of mercy
c. Seeds of joy
d. Seeds of peace
e. Seeds of charity

4. Powerful prayers:

a. Meditation — Our Lady of Sorrows Rosary
b. Healing — Chaplet of Divine Mercy

c. Reconciliation — Holy Sacrifice of the Mass, Exposition of the Blessed Sacrament
d. Unification (Man to God and person to person) — Sacrament of Reconciliation, Sacrament of Holy Eucharist.

Finally, she put down her pen, knowing that the thoughts she had expressed on paper could not possibly be her own, but must certainly have been inspired by God.

It was a blue-print for Christian living, she suddenly realised.

Going down on her knees, Sylvia prayed for the strength and courage to follow it.

The journey was a long one, but typically, Fr Peter Rookey didn't find it so. Arriving in the Philippines, he felt extraordinarily exhilarated at this, the beginning of a healing pilgrimage that would run from October 11th to October 30th, 1993. Now he understood why Pope John Paul knelt down to kiss the ground when he first stepped on new soil.

The islands were beautiful, even breath-taking, set as they were off the coast of southeast Asia, between Formosa and Indonesia. There were said to be over seven thousand altogether, he recalled, some of them more rocky islets than anything else. His visits would take him to some of the largest, from Luzon in the north of the group to Mindanao in the south.

He was in the tropics here, a place of hot sunshine and torrential rainfall, of violent typhoons and occasional earthquakes. A land of active volcanoes which dominated those areas in which they were found, like the volcano mountain of Mayon in southern Luzon which was said to be crowned at night with a fiery glow. From the forests in these islands came some of the finest hardwood timber found anywhere in the world.

Jesus would have been busy here, Fr Peter thought suddenly, recalling the Lord's thirty years as a carpenter.

The twenty days that followed on these islands were, he later admitted, among some of the happiest and most inspirational of his life.

The welcome he received humbled him, a genuine welcome everywhere he went from the poorest Filipinos to those in positions of power and wealth. To each person he gave the same blessing, and the Good News that Jesus was alive, Jesus was love, Jesus wanted to heal all their ills, from the spiritual to the emotional, to the physical.

Everywhere he went, they came in their thousands to see the man with healing in his hands. And always he taught them that it was not he who healed, but the great and loving Saviour whose lowly servant he was.

And as he celebrated the Mass and prayed and blessed them with holy oil and with the crucifix he carried everywhere, miracles happened. As in so many places, the blind received their sight, the deaf heard and those with terminal illness professed a healing experience.

From the modern cities with their tall buildings, busy offices and beautiful homes, to the villages of small wooden houses, sliding shutters and thatched roofs, the people came to see the man their newspapers, television and radio stations had told them about. Few went away untouched by the power of his message and his ministry.

He was moved to tears on many occasions by the faith and joy of the people. By the poor who brought their sick with such open and child-like expectation, and by the loving acceptance of his brother priests.

One experience remained imprinted for ever on the minds of those who travelled with Fr Peter over these weeks.

It happened when a hospital chaplain in Metro Manila invited him to administer the Sacrament of the Healing of the Sick to twenty-five ICU patients under his care. The invitation was blocked several times by a director of the hospital, but finally permission was granted.

Going from one room to the next, Fr Peter performed the Last Rites with love and humility, blessing each person with the Holy Oil and with his crucifix containing the relics of the Servite saints.

He then ended each anointing by kissing the feet of each terminally ill patient.

The experience was a deep and moving one for the people who accompanied him, each of whom spoke afterwards of the wave of sanctity they felt, the promise of a happy death at the beginning of each patient's journey to the place Jesus had gone to prepare for them.

That night, four patients had made their eternal crossover to new life. Before Fr Peter left for the United States the Chaplain thanked him for the lesson he had learned in helping the terminally ill. And told him that already, two-thirds of the people he had blessed had gone home to God with peace and happiness.

Praying one evening, in anticipation of the night's healing Mass, he watched as the spirit of his creator painted one of the glorious sunsets for which the city is famous across Manila Bay. And he thanked God for the love and the peace and the joy of so much spiritual beauty he had experienced during his weeks on the island, and for the healings of body, spirit and mind that Jesus had allowed him the privilege of witnessing.

He now had little trouble in understanding the stories he had heard, of the bloodless coup that had occurred in these islands attributed, he had been told by Cardinal Sin to his call to the two million Catholics to come out of their homes and onto the streets and pray the Rosary. The wall of prayer that had followed had stopped the tanks and led to the bloodless ousting of former President Marcos.

What a wonderful place in which to have spent his 78th birthday.

He had lost count of the number of places he had been, the people he had met and prayed with. Somebody had reminded him just the previous evening. Four cathedrals, nine churches, three cloistered monasteries, three prison chapels, two hospitals, three Marian centres and a home for unwed mothers. And no, he had assured those who asked him, he did not feel tired. In fact, he felt renewed.

And although he never made demands on the Lord, but simply followed where He led, he wondered if perhaps it was in His plans that one day his servant Peter might return to these islands.

The young priest picked up the newspaper and opened it. He didn't know quite why he was doing this. It was the first newspaper he had read in eighteen months since the crisis he had been experiencing in his vocation had come to a head.

He had questioned every aspect of his priestly status then, and struggled daily with his apostasy in the church. Finally, he had become totally rebellious, refusing to perform his duties and falling into what he knew was an aggressive, depressive attitude.

He had left the church then, withdrawing without permission and hurting his family bitterly in the process.

The last eighteen months had been the worst Fr Robert had ever experienced, as slowly his emotional state declined.

One day, in what he can only describe as a sane moment, it dawned on him that if God truly wanted him to work in His vineyard, He would give him two signs.

The first sign he asked was that his Bishop would permit him to talk to him personally.

The second sign would be that he would somehow find a foreign priest who would heal all his spiritual brokenness.

He had waited for a year before his Bishop had entered into dialogue with him. The tearful reunion both had experienced at this meeting had washed away some of his guilt.

He turned the newspaper pages and a picture and headlines suddenly caught his eye. Fr Peter Rookey, a priest from Chicago, USA was here, in the Philippines!

Surely this could only be an answer from God, the promise that his second wished-for sign had been granted?

"I was overwhelmed with joy about this," he recalls emotionally.

"I boarded a ten-hour bus ride from Batan to Betis, Pampanga to meet this priest. But like many pilgrims I waited in vain for six hours at Our Lady of the Rosary church that Friday 21st October, 1993. There had been difficulties and Fr Rookey would not be coming."

His heart sank, but reaching into his pocket he found the newspaper clipping that included Fr Peter's schedule. The next available opportunity for him to meet the American priest, he discovered, would be the following Tuesday 25th where he was scheduled to visit a home for unwed mothers.

"This meant I had to swallow my pride," he recalls.

"To meet Fr Rookey I would have to beg lodgings at my favourite uncle's home in Manila."

Lodgings were not refused, but his uncle's family gave him what he calls 'the silent treatment'.

"I can't blame them for that," he says.

"They too had suffered loss of face for my rebellious actions. But it was a humbling experience to be ignored by those who had always been so friendly to me in the past."

Deep in his heart, he says, he knew that his quest to see Fr Rookey would be rewarded.

"The next Tuesday I arrived at the Home and explained my desire to see Fr Rookey. The assistant director was sympathetic to my cause and gave me a hearty breakfast and a private room to do my meditation.

"Later, I went to the area that had been prepared for the Holy Mass, placing myself in a corner to remain unnoticed.

"A lady came over to me and introduced herself as having travelled with Fr Rookey. She wanted to know if I needed private time with him. I raised my pleading eyes to her. She smiled so tenderly, which melted away my fears. In a childlike manner I said, 'yes'."

The woman took his hand and led him through the crowd that had gathered, telling him that he was welcome to concelebrate with Fr Rookey, and that an extra alb was ready for him.

"I felt so good," he recalls through his tears.

"My thorn — the guilt I had been carrying for so long — seemed to have been taken off my chest."

That day, he says, he began again knowing having talked with Fr Peter that his Father in heaven had truly forgiven him, that he had been given the gift of new life and that everything would now be in place for him.

"And I give thanks to Our Lady of Sorrows for my reception and welcome back into the vineyard of God the Father, God the Son, God the Holy Spirit, through my brother priest, Rev Fr Peter Mary Rookey of the Order of the Servants of Mary."

Chapter Thirteen

LIFELINE TO HEAVEN

'Dear Fr Rookey,

Our Lord was in you as you walked, healing the sick. I have never seen so many miracles in my life. A little boy deaf from birth healed... a young crippled girl running and jumping about happily... a young girl about 16 years old who wore thick glasses all her life healed.

You asked us to say the Rosary. Not just that. I felt the real presence of Our Lord and Our Lady.

May the Lord and His holy Mother bless and watch over you. I thank you for everything you did for four thousand people. I do write from the heart and I thank you on behalf of all, from my heart.

Yours very sincerely.' (England)

The rest of the family were still sleeping when Kathy awoke. It was the sun that had wakened her, she decided, her alarm clock showing a full hour before she needed to get up. Lying there, she looked at the top branches of the tree that could be seen from her bedroom window. And the memories of the day before flooded back into her mind.

How could she have forgotten, she wondered? Perhaps it was because she had lived so long with the weight of Tim's addiction to alcohol. And the unbearable misery it had meant for the entire family these last six years.

It had been worse for the children, she believed. They had grown ashamed of their father — and fearful of him when the whiskey took over his personality and the gentle, kind young man she had married turned into a violent animal.

That was how the kids had described him, as one by one they had moved out of home. An animal — the only word, they said, for somebody who showed no human feelings of kindness, love or consideration.

Turning her head to look at his sleeping face on the pillow beside her, Kathy's heart ached for the loss to them both of the man he had once been. And despite the pain and humiliation she had suffered over these years, somehow she had never stopped loving him. Not even when his drinking had become so bad that losing all sense he had lashed out at her, knocking her across the kitchen where she fell, fracturing her wrist and badly bruising her face.

"It's a disease — and if he had something like cancer I wouldn't leave him," she told her mother and her children, when they had suggested separation as the only sensible thing.

And she truly believed that his addiction to alcoholism was a disease, one that was destroying him physically and mentally.

It had begun while he was working, and had accelerated when he was made redundant. The habit of dropping into the pub with the lads after work had been a hard one to break. For a time he continued to meet some of his former colleagues each evening, just to hear what was going on, he explained to Kathy. Maybe they would know of some job that was going. But of course, they never did and finally Tim began to avoid them, embarrassed because he no longer had the money to keep up the heavy drinking they enjoyed so much.

So he had started going out on his own, to buy the evening newspaper he said, and see whether there were any jobs being advertised. Maybe that was true at the beginning, Kathy thought, but the real reason was more than likely the fact that drink helped him forget the way life had turned sour. That at fifty-one he was too old to go back into the national workforce as unemployment figures reached new heights.

Down at the local pub he was one of the lads, many of whom were also unemployed. And as the night wore on the drinking got heavier, the laughter louder and the money that was so desperately needed for the household flew into the landlord's till while Kathy frantically tried to make ends meet.

All three kids were in college then — and all three left home as soon as their studies were finished, because they just couldn't live with their father.

Only Kathy had stayed, hoping against hope that one day there would be a miracle and life would once again be something to enjoy, rather than to fear.

And she had been right. Last night there had been a miracle. She just knew it. It might take time to materialise properly, but it had happened.

Slipping out of bed to go downstairs and make herself a cup of tea, her mind went over the events of the last couple of days.

She had never been much into prayer groups, although her friend Pamela had tried to interest her in the group she attended. In fact, if she was to be truthful, she only continued to go to Mass because she felt that if she gave that up she would be cutting herself off from the source of miracles. And miracles she believed in.

She'd read a book, once, about a so-called healing nun. When she went about praying for people in front of the Blessed Sacrament miracles happened, and even those who were terminally ill were healed. She had been very struck by the content of the book, but it had never occurred to her to ask God directly for a miracle. What she needed, she had decided, was to find a healer, like the nun in question, who would ask God for a miracle for Tim.

Pamela had come to see her two days earlier. Luckily Tim was out when she called. He didn't like Pamela ever since she had given him a piece of her mind when Kathy's wrist had been fractured. But he'd been wary of her, especially when Pamela said that the next time something like that happened she would telephone the police herself and Tim could explain his behaviour straight to them.

"Look," she had said to Kathy, as she held up a newspaper. "There's a healing priest coming to Manchester. Didn't you say that you believed in miracles?"

Pamela had sat down and read the newspaper feature. The priest was from America. His name was Fr Peter Rookey and he was in England on his second visit that year, the previous one having been in January.

"Reading this newspaper article, how this priest was well known for curing people when he prayed with them, I decided that nothing was going to stop me from going to see him and ask him to pray for Tim.

"I didn't ask Tim to come with me. I knew that was out of the question. He would have been furious. He had never admitted that he had a problem with alcohol, even when the kids threw it in his face.

"But I really believed that if I asked for a miracle, Tim would be healed.

"Looking back, that seems so childish. Maybe if I'd had time to sit down and think about it, I'd never have gone. Reason would have taken over. But as it was, the healing service was the next day. So I just decided to go."

She was surprised by the crowds who had come to see the priest, she says. And she never got to have that talk with Fr Peter. "But as the priest explained to us what would happen at the service, I realised that I didn't need to talk to him.

"He told us how we could stand in proxy for another person. That our faith was sufficient for those who had not been able to come. That we could bring our children or our parents, or husbands, wives or friends to the Lord, and receive the blessing in their name.

"When it came time for the laying on of hands, I didn't dash straight up, as I had thought I would. Instead, Pamela and myself sat there and watched all that was happening for at least twenty minutes. I think even Pamela was taken aback by what she saw. Even in her prayer group she had never experienced anything like this.

"I was really made speechless when a woman who had been in a wheelchair suddenly stood up at the priest's invitation and began to walk. Her daughter or friend who had been pushing the chair began to cry, and so did the woman. The priest told the woman to push her chair out and away through the crowd, and she did. It was really emotional.

"Then a younger woman began to cry when her little son, who was also in a wheelchair, stood up and walked. He kept turning to his mother and looking up at her in amazement, then looking back down at his legs as if he couldn't believe they were carrying him. The mother just broke her heart crying and I don't think there was anybody else there who wasn't crying also.

"Some of the people looked so ill. Many had obviously had chemotherapy and had lost their hair and were so waxy or yellow coloured. But even they seemed to walk straighter after Fr Rookey had prayed with them.

"The thing that really surprised me was that once he had prayed over somebody, and even if they had a seemingly miraculous healing like getting out of a wheelchair and walking, Fr Rookey just moved on to the next person. He took absolutely no glory for what was happening and that really impressed me."

Finally, Kathy says, she and Pamela took their turn with those waiting to be blessed. As she waited for the priest to approach her, Kathy says that she felt ill and shaky.

"I had put so much faith in this healing working, but now that the moment had arrived I suddenly began to have doubts. Part of me wanted to run away. I remember my legs beginning to shake and my mouth going really dry, so that when Fr Rookey came up to me and asked me if I was ill, I tried to answer him but couldn't for a few moments.

"Then I was afraid that he would walk on by and I suddenly burst out with 'It's my husband, Father, he's an alcoholic. He's very bad. My children have all left home.'

"I remember him taking my arm as if to steady me, and then he held his other hand up over me with the crucifix in it, and he began to pray. He seemed to be there for ages, although I had seen him pray only a very short time with others. Pamela was beside me and she said it was several minutes. Some of it I don't remember, other things he said I do. He was asking God to reward my faith in coming here to plead for my husband. I remember wondering how he knew I had faith that Tim would be healed.

"He prayed for my husband, although not by name as I hadn't told him Tim's name. He just kept referring to 'this lovely daughter's husband' asking God to heal him of his addiction and bring peace and healing to the entire family. Then he placed his hands on my head and I felt as if my body was tingling all over. It was the strangest sensation I have ever experienced — it felt almost as if a small electric current had gone right through my body. I felt warm all over, light — as if I weighed nothing, as if I could sort of float away — and all the fear and the tension and the pressure that I had lived with for the last years just seemed unimportant any more. I remember feeling as if I was swaying. I think I did sway back, because I felt hands behind me. Then I seemed to straighten up again. This happened twice, and then I think I just stood there for ages, with my eyes closed as if I was half asleep, but feeling more relaxed than I had ever felt in my life.

"I don't even remember Fr Rookey moving away from me. In fact, the next thing I was aware of was turning to go back to my seat and almost tripping over Pamela who was lying on the ground beside me.

"She'd had this resting in the spirit, that Fr Rookey had explained to us could happen. She told me afterwards that it was the most peaceful and beautiful experience she had ever had in her life. She was only sorry that I hadn't experienced the same thing, but you know, I think I did, only I didn't fall down.

"And when I went back to my seat, I truly believed that Tim would be healed."

On their way into the service, Kathy says, she and Pamela were handed little cards with Fr Peter Rookey's picture on one side and the Miracle Prayer on the other.

"Back in my seat I just kept looking at this prayer and saying it in my mind. For some reason it seemed awfully important, and I made a promise to myself then, that I would say it every day, not just for Tim but for myself and the kids too.

"I hadn't been a great Catholic. And I'd really been a worse Christian I suppose. I just hadn't given God much time in my life, except to continue going to Mass. But there had been no feeling in it, as if He was so far away, He wasn't real.

"But that night I knew in myself that He is real. And that He loves me. He loves us all."

The next morning when she woke up, Kathy says, she expected to witness a sudden dramatic healing.

"But Tim didn't seem any different. He was quieter, but he still left the house that night. I sat there in front of the television, not really seeing it, and feeling suddenly very tired and depressed. Then I thought of the Miracle Prayer and I went upstairs, took it from my handbag, and began to say it."

She was in bed when Tim came in that night. Strangely, he was less noisy, more in control of himself, she thought. Pamela had telephoned her during the evening.

'Don't worry,' she had said. 'I have a strange feeling that everything is going to be okay.'

The next day he didn't go out to the pub until it was almost closing time. Kathy stopped herself from asking why. Best to leave him to God, she thought.

Over the days that followed he went out less and less, usually coming home sober, a fact that seemed to surprise him more than her. And he took to sitting down to watching television with her, and then to giving her a help around the house, to making a start on the garden which was wild and unkempt because Kathy hadn't had the heart to do more than cut the lawn for a long time past.

He wasn't drinking at home either, she suddenly realised. The whiskey bottle in the livingroom cabinet was almost half full. And he began to talk to her.

"One day he admitted to me that he realised now he'd had a problem with drink. And he asked me to help him. He said he felt it had destroyed his life, but that there were times when he just couldn't resist going down to the pub and drinking some more.

"So I suggested Alcoholics Anonymous and I told him that we'd both go, to support one another."

That was over a year ago. Tim's fight against his addiction hasn't been an easy one, Kathy admits. And there were times when it broke through and he hit the bottle again for a couple of days.

But the worst is over, she feels. He's now almost ten months without a drink, he's sleeping well and he's got involved in local community voluntary work. And best of all, they've discussed those terrible years openly, which Kathy feels is a huge part of the healing process.

"I was right," she says now.

"Miracles are possible. And I still say that Miracle Prayer every day. It's like a lifeline to heaven."

She's never seen Fr Rookey since, she says, but every day she includes him in her prayers.

"I feel as if I once met a saint. God must love him very much to work through him so powerfully."

Chapter Fourteen

THE PRESENCE OF MARY

'Dear Fr Rookey,

On Tuesday October 4th, I had an appointment with my doctor. After looking at the CAT scan pictures of my left lung he told me he was 89% sure I had cancer and if I waited for a year it would be too late for surgery. I agreed to have the surgery the following Tuesday, October 11th.

On October 6th I attended a healing prayer service at the Visitation of Our Lady Church in Louisiana. The service was conducted by Fr Peter Mary Rookey OSM of Chicago, Illinois. The replica statue of the Blessed Mother (from Medjugorje) was unveiled during the Mass.

I went to the front of the church by the altar and stood close to the new statue of Mary. She was so beautiful I could not stop looking at her. I was crying all the time I was looking at her.

Father Rookey was praying over the sick. When he reached me, a feeling I cannot describe went through my body. It was like I had lost all control of my body and I fell backwards. I had the feeling, afterwards, that I had been healed and that when it came time for the surgery the doctor wouldn't find any trace of cancer.

I was admitted to the Medical Centre on Sunday, October 9th. On Monday October 10th I was on my way to have x-rays taken of my chest. On my way to the x-ray department I told the orderly they weren't going to find anything wrong. He said he hoped I was right.

On Tuesday October 11th, after my surgery, the doctor came in the waiting room where my friends and family were. They said he had a puzzled look on his face, as if he could not believe what had happened. He told them that the surgery went well. There was no cancer. All they found was a fungus growing on the outside of my lung.

The day the doctor discharged me from the hospital, I told him what had happened at the healing service and showed him a picture of the statue of the Blessed Mother. He said it was good to have faith like that.

I believed in prayers before, but since my healing experience my belief and faith is stronger than ever.' (Louisiana)

You have a great devotion to Our Lady.

It's more a statement, than a question, but glancing into the rear view mirror as we drive to the office of the International Compassion Ministry in Olympia Fields off Chicago's Governors Highway, Fr Peter decides to answer it anyway.

"Oh well, I wouldn't be much of a Servant of Mary if I didn't.

"That's our official title you know, we Servites. I heard those words impressed upon me very strongly — I don't know if by inner locution or what — several years ago when I was in Medjugorje. I was in the choir loft of the church during the appearance of Our Lady to the visionaries there and these words struck me so strongly that I just don't know how to describe it, from the psalms and in Latin, 'Behold, I am your servant, the servant of your handmaid. You have loosed my bonds.' And this of course is Mary. She has played a vital role in the spiritual lives of mankind. And in this healing ministry I am constantly asking Our Beautiful Lady to touch Jesus to obtain this healing, whatever it is. Her word is command for Him you know."

He has been many times to Medjugorje, where for thirteen years there have been reports of the Virgin's daily apparitions to a specially chosen group of young people.

Does he believe that the events taking place there are important to people's faith?

"Oh yes, I can not deny what I have seen there. In Medjugorje Our Lady is calling us back to Jesus, to worship of Jesus in the Eucharist, to Adoration, to prayer — three hours a day she asks for and she recommends especially the Rosary. And that makes sense, particularly for the healing ministry because if I don't pray two or three hours a day, then nothing will happen when I lay hands on people to ask for their healing. It's like trying to write a cheque when you don't have money in the bank. It will just bounce back in your face."

How does he find three hours to pray when every day is busier than the other?

He just makes the time, he says.

"Because I know this other work is useless without it."

He generally prays for two hours first thing each morning, rising as early as is necessary to have the time before his busy schedule begins, and despite the fact that he may only have got to bed in the early hours of the same morning.

"And the Lord sometimes gets me up in the middle of the night to pray, but I'm so weak that after I have prayed I go back to bed!" he laughs.

"I think He wants me to pray through the night too, but you know I'm like my namesake Peter. 'Would you not watch one hour with me,' the Lord had to ask him, so I guess I'm well named in more than one way."

He can get by on fairly little sleep he admits. It's not unusual for him to get to bed at 2am — having returned from a healing Mass and said his night prayers — then get up again at 5am to pray for two hours before saying Mass at 7am. He likes to pray the Office before Mass, he explains.

His times in Medjugorje have been truly moments of prayer and joy, he says, with the presence of Mary so tangible in the valley.

"I can not deny that when I go to Medjugorje, marvellous things happen there at the healing services, especially when we have been there around June 24th, the anniversary time. In those days, Our Lady seems to be especially generous in obtaining graces for those who are ill or who seek her intercession."

The memories flood through his mind as the traffic flows past us.

The 14 year old German boy who had only 3% vision in one eye and was blind in the other, and who recovered his sight when Fr Peter blessed him in the fields behind the house in which he was staying.

The numbers of pilgrims reporting cancer who wrote to him afterwards to tell of their doctor's amazement at the results of new tests.

The deaf child who heard and the dumb child who spoke.

He didn't need to explain the scenes to me. I had been in Medjugorje with Fr Peter on several occasions and had witnessed many such events for myself.

Why did he think Our Lady came to Medjugorje, I ask him as the car turns in towards the building that houses the small ministry office?

"I think the reason is obvious," he replies.

"She wanted to warn us, as our mother.

"There are words in the Scriptures that I think explain it all. Such as those of St Paul when he said the Lord sends us His prophets. Or the parable that Jesus told about how the man sent his servants to the winepress to get his share of the produce. But other servants there treated them terribly and even killed some of them. So the man sent his heir, his only son, saying they will surely respect him. But they killed him also.

"Well, now I think that what has happened in the last century is that He has been sending His Mother in the hope that we will listen to her beautiful approach."

He stops the car in front of a modern office building. When I had first visited Fr Peter in Chicago in February 1990 he was based in St Dominic's priory in the city, right across the street from Cabrini Green, one of the worst ghetto areas in Chicago.

"You sure you want to go there?" the cab driver had asked me when I gave him my destination.

"That's not a safe place for you, lady. They lean out the windows round there and shoot people who get lost and stray in. Why only the other day there was a lady murdered on one of the corners and last month there were at least four murders there that I know of. And if you don't get murdered, more than likely you'll get mugged or raped."

It hadn't been an attractive picture he'd painted, but my desire to meet up again with Fr Peter was stronger than my fear of what terrors Cabrini Green might hold. Yes, I assured him, I wanted to go there.

"Well okay, I'll take you, seeing as you're a stranger here and I wouldn't like to see anything happen. Generally it's the sort of place where we taxi drivers just won't go, or if we do we put the boot down and just drive through there no matter what gets in our way, but I'll take you."

He had stopped the cab some distance from Cabrini Green and asked for the fare. He would take me on to St Dominic's priory, he told me, but he wouldn't be hanging around there, and the fare as far as here was good enough.

When he dropped me off then shot away with a screech of tyres before I had time to find my bearings, I was less brave. Several youths hanging round a street corner nearby came walking towards me. The buildings were the run-down tenement type that I had seen in some films. And when I rang the doorbell to St Dominic's, nobody answered.

It seemed like an eternity before the door opened and by that time quite a crowd of youths had gathered. Fr Peter's welcoming hug was never more appreciated.

Later, showing me through the church of St Dominic's, he pointed out bullet holes in the stained glass.

"Oh, it's a tough old area right enough, but it's not the worst," he said. And later again he took me down the street to a coffee shop. Recalling the taxi driver's warnings I was less than enthusiastic about going, but very glad later that I did.

Seeing Fr Peter here, among some of the poorest and most marginalised in the city, I was struck by his genuine love for all, rich or poor, black or white. Outside one partially boarded-up building — a pub as I discovered when we came closer — were about a dozen children, their tough, hard looking little faces belying their years. Yet, at the touch of

Fr Peter's hand on their heads, they replied to his cheery hello with smiles that softened their features.

"God bless you now," he said to everyone we met, shaking hands, blessing them briefly as he passed, smiling at all. I kept close to him, resisting the urge to hang out of his habit in case we got separated. And then felt ashamed of my fear in the face of what were only the results of poverty and deprivation.

The building we were entering now was worlds away from Cabrini Green I thought, as we took the lift to the office that Fr Peter had been persuaded to accept at a very small rent from a business woman who thought the world of both him and his ministry.

After he had been moved from St Dominic's when the church was closed, along with many others in the city due to poor attendance, lack of funds and a decline of Catholics in the area, Fr Peter had gone first to another Servite community for six months before being moved again to St Bonfilious' priory. One of the problems however was that unlike St Dominic's priory, there was no room for an office for Fr Peter's ministry. And when you receive thousands of telephone calls and letters in a year, an office is vital if you are to meet the needs of so many people in search of help, counselling and healing.

The other problem, even when after much prayer and discussion he took up the offer of the office in Olympia Fields, was who was going to run it?

In St Dominic's he had relied heavily on the help of Sr Caran, a retired nun who tried to cope with the flood of mail and telephone calls and the compiling of Fr Peter's schedule and calendar, which were also sent out to people all over the world to keep them informed about the International

Compassion Ministry, and to assist them in keeping the Ministry and Fr Peter in their prayers.

Sr Caran made valiant efforts to travel to the Olympia Fields office once or twice a week, but it was a marathon journey involving bus and train and then a cab or a lift from the train station, and the same in reverse later that day. The office depended on volunteers, most of whom could only give a small amount of time each week, and who had to fit in that work with their family responsibilities.

"But God always sends us the people we need to help do his work," Fr Peter maintains.

And he has no doubt whatsoever that God sent him Brother Jim Hrechko.

Chapter Fifteen

A HELPING HAND

Brother Jim Hrechko's first meeting with Fr Peter came about in the way most people meet Father — when they go to seek his help.

Jim (as he then was before joining the Servite Brothers) attended a prayer group which Fr Peter visited as one of a number of priests who came to give the 'laying on of hands'. Shortly afterwards, when his middle son returned home from California a full-blown alcoholic and addict — he sought out Fr Peter to ask his advise and his prayers.

It was a meeting that was to result in a deep personal friendship between the two men, and a huge amount of healing for Jim's son.

A widower, Jim Hrechko began to visit Fr Peter at St Dominic's, taking his car to the train station then the train into Chicago city where Fr Peter would pick him up and take him to the priory. The two men would then sit in the rectory kitchen and talk for hours.

It wasn't long before Jim was volunteering to help with the office work in the ministry. It began with one day a week, he smiles wryly now, but ended up with his taking complete charge of the new office in Olympia Fields. A former office manager before his retirement, he was a god-send to the ministry which was growing all the time as invitations poured in for Fr Peter to visit countries throughout the world, not to mention states right across America.

Could he not have found something less arduous to do with his retirement than take on a full-time unpaid position running an office? Brother Jim doesn't see it that way. His work in the International Compassion Ministry he says, is a privilege, to be close to a man whose 'every action, every thought is love. Fr Peter is love itself,' he says simply.

As the demands grew on the ministry, Brother Jim pointed out to Fr Peter that the time had come to take on a full-time paid worker. It would be unfair to expect anyone to work full-time in a voluntary position, pointed out the man who was doing just that!

It took some time before they received approval from the Servite order to do this, "but I guess the Lord wanted us to wait that long so we could find the right person," Br Jim laughs.

Her name was Margaret Ward, known as Marje, married with several teenage children, a director of the youth ministry in her parish — and a wizard on the computer!

Marje has proved to be a real blessing to the ministry office, Br Jim points out, which grew so much again over the last couple of years that they needed the help of extra volunteers.

Every letter that comes into the International Compassion Ministry is placed before Fr Peter, who reads each one before writing notes for a reply. All requests for prayer are noted in a special 'Prayer' book, so that nobody is ever forgotten and, most touching of all, Fr Peter prays over each letter, asking God's healing and blessing on those who sent it and those for whom they wrote.

Jim remembers the day he first discovered Fr Peter's practice regarding the letters.

"We were in southern Illinois for two healing Masses, travelling from one parish to the other. When we arrived at the second parish we had two hours to spare before the Mass began. Wherever we go, Father brings the most recent letters with him, to read over them. He told me that he wanted to finish reading some of these, so I left him alone at the desk in the rectory and went for a walk to pray the Rosary outside.

"When I returned and went looking for Father, I found that the chair had been pushed back from the desk and Fr Rookey was on his knees, praying over the letters. And when he looked up at me, all he said, with tears in his eyes, was 'These letters are so touching'."

The letters, Br Jim confirms, come from all over the world where Fr Peter has visited or where newspaper or television reports have brought word of his ministry. From England and Ireland, Scotland and Wales, from all over Europe and right across the United States. From Africa, Australia, the Philippines and from South America, where Fr Peter was so overwhelmed by the faith of the people during a visit to Mexico and by their devotion to the Eucharist which they came forward on their knees to accept.

Br Jim is also the man who is entrusted by the Servite Order to handle the awkward subject of finance. Fr Peter has a strict vow of poverty — even the bedroom in which he sleeps contains only a bed, a table and a hard-backed upright chair in place of the upholstered easy chair that was there when he first moved in.

In a society which has been shaken by the financial exploits of some of the Hollywood-style evangelists, Br Jim is a man of integrity and honour who ensures that any money that comes in to the ministry, in the form of donations, offerings for Masses and so on, is fully documented. Each month, the sum of money that has been designated by the Servite Order to cover the ministry expenses — postage, paper, Marje's salary, the monthly calendar which has a mailing list of almost seven thousand, and Fr Peter's own contribution to the priory house in which he lives (all travelling expenses are met by the people who issue invitations to Fr Peter to travel to hold healing Masses in their country or area) — is met, then any surplus given into the Servite general funds to help further their work all over the world.

The friendship that has grown up between Fr Peter Rookey and Br Jim Hrechko is one based on deep Christian love and respect. Without Br Jim's support the ministry would not have been able to spread its wings, I suspect. Br Jim disagrees.

"The Lord will always find a way to progress His work," he says.

"Father needed somebody to help him — and I was there.

"Every day, during my prayer and contemplation, I thank the Lord for my time with Fr Peter — and I ask Him that if it is His will, I will be left to continue with Father for as long as possible.

"Working with Fr Peter had been a wonderful, a humbling, but also a very uplifting experience. I have been privileged to see the power of God in action on so many occasions, and I have been left in awe at times of the deep love of Christ for us all, Who not only laid down His life for us, but despite that supreme sacrifice still continues to call us to Him each day."

Chapter Sixteen

A SMALL WHITE BIRD

'Dear Fr Rookey,

During one of your healing Masses in Kansas in August, I prayed for a reconciliation with my father. The next day we took a small step toward that reconciliation.

For ten years my father and I have had a rocky relationship, sometimes even violent. So that small step was a very important part of a healing in our family. My father and I are still having our difficulties now and then, but that's pretty normal with two stubborn mules in one household. However, we are making progress little by little and I am very grateful for it.

Another thing I would like to thank you for is bringing me back to Catholicism. I've only been a Catholic for four years. I graduated from a Catholic High School. I was disillusioned with Catholicism and was losing my faith. It seemed to me that the Church didn't care for the little people. Keep in mind that I was (and still am, pretty much) a young and impressionable teenager, so every disappointment was multiplied tenfold. I had asked my parish for help several times and was always turned away with: 'I don't know how to help you. Goodbye'.

When I went to your healing Mass and saw you do a two-hour Mass, then hang around afterwards talking to people until everyone was gone, I was surprised. I had never seen a priest do that before. You really cared for the people. I realised the Church isn't as bad as I thought. I knew there were many Catholics (priests, nuns, lay people, parishioners) who would do anything for people in need. I just wanted to stick with my faith. So I decided to give Catholicism a chance. Now I'm attending a Catholic college and I wouldn't go anywhere else.

I have my father back and my faith. I thank you from the bottom of my heart Fr Rookey.' (Kansas)

The ravages of war have changed the face of Bosnia-Herzegovina and prevented all but a few pilgrims making their way to the place where the Mother of God has been appearing for thirteen years. Despite that war, Fr Peter Rookey has continued to visit Medjugorje in the company of a small number of people from the United States and latterly from Ireland. They have been quieter and more peaceful pilgrimages for him, the valley that once teemed with thousands from all over the world now strangely empty, allowing Fr Peter to have special time alone, praying in the church or in the beautiful little chapel of Adoration, saying the Stations of the Cross and being visibly renewed by the undoubted presence of Jesus and Mary.

Medjugorje, the place where the Mother of God has chosen to come and call the world back to her Son, holds a special place in the heart of this Servant of Mary. Over the years of his pilgrimages there, it has been the scene of some wonderful physical and spiritual healings in his ministry.

One of those that comes to his mind is the story of Virginia Landy from Rhode Island.

For two years, Virginia had been battling with a mysterious illness that was eventually diagnosed as multiple sclerosis and which left her facing life from a wheelchair. Following tests and treatment, her doctors told her not to expect a cure, that the best they could do was slow down the progress of the disease.

Joining a support group that met every second week near her home, she found comfort and solidarity among others in the same position.

Although brought up a Catholic, Virginia had strayed from the Church, while still maintaining her own contact with God. Which made her decision to visit Medjugorje all the more astonishing to her friends and family when she announced her intention to them to do just this.

It wasn't just a matter of booking a flight she discovered however, when undaunted by all opposition she went ahead with her plans. Most travel agencies didn't want to take the responsibility of sending a client in a wheelchair on the long and difficult journey to the remote valley between the mountains in Bosnia-Herzegovina. Undaunted, Virginia talked her sister-in-law into travelling with her.

It was a trip she will never forget, stopping as they did en route in Rome, where they attended an audience with Pope John Paul II. Placed in the section reserved especially for those in wheelchairs, Virginia was overjoyed when the Pope walked up to her, clasped both her hands, then placed his hand on her head in blessing before moving on.

It was June 23rd 1991 when she first arrived in Medjugorje, the day before the tenth anniversary of the first apparition of the Mother of God. Along with over one hundred thousand people, Virginia and her sister-in-law joined in the local Croatian Mass, during which the apparition of Our Lady took place. Later, they heard that an American priest was holding a healing service in one of the two huge green tents that had been pitched down behind the church. It had been no easy task to push the wheelchair down the stony path towards the tents, the wheels constantly sinking into the ground or refusing to budge over the stones. Eventually, they made it and Virginia was led into the section at the front reserved for wheelchairs. There were about five hundred people in the tent at the time, and as Virginia listened to the Chicago priest Fr Peter Rookey whom she had never met before, speak about God's healing power in the lives of mankind, she began to cry, feeling unworthy to be there with so many who were obviously deeply devoted to the practice of their religion.

Fr Rookey walked past Virginia soon afterwards, moving down the line to bless those in wheelchairs with the crucifix he held in his hand, then returning to stop in front of her.

Did she believe in the power of Jesus to heal her, he asked?

She had no doubt of her answer 'Yes'.

"Silver and gold have I not, but what I have I give you," the priest said to her.

"In the name of Jesus, get up and walk."

And in front of the astonished eyes of her sister -in-law and the others in the group, Virginia stood up, stepped away from her wheelchair and walked.

At home she had been able to take one or two shuffling steps, when necessary, but this was different. Her back was straight, she later pointed out to others and she wasn't shuffling, but walking normally. And later, her heart full of joy and wonder, she climbed the hill of Podbrdo, where the Madonna had first appeared to the young visionaries, and thanked God for the healing she believed she had experienced.

Back home a couple of weeks later, her doctor told her that from a medical point of view he believed that she still had multiple sclerosis. But what he couldn't explain, pointed out Virginia, was how she was walking when three doctors had told her she never would, and how she had no pain.

The story made headline news in the local newspaper as Virginia joyfully returned to the centre where she had once been a patient, to visit and help the friends she had made there. Her doctor had refused to be interviewed about the matter, but the pastor of her church when questioned about the reported miraculous healing, had seen no reason why somebody who had experienced a healing should not share the wonderful news with others.

It's a view Fr Peter would agree with. Praise for himself is something this humble and deeply-spiritual priest will never accept, but praise for the God he represents is another matter.

And at every Mass or healing service he encourages those present to come forward and give honour and glory to God for the wonderful things He has done in their lives.

"Don't be like the nine lepers that walked away without thanking the Lord," he says.

"Come and give praise and thanks to God."

As the hot mid-day sun beats down, Fr Peter Rookey sits on a wooden bench in front of the church of St James, a small glass of water in his hand from the nearby tap his only break with the day long fast he maintains. Most people have gone indoors to rest and find relief from the burning sun that fills the valley of Medjugorje with languor. Until this moment, Fr Peter has been surrounded by people seeking prayer, confession and consolation. Only now does he have time to rest awhile before joining yet another group for prayers and healing.

Some of the other healings that have been reported following his prayers here in this valley run through my mind. The young woman in her early thirties who had only minimal sight, but who declared that she could see following Fr Peter's blessing — and the tremor of excitement that had run through the praying pilgrims at her words.

The thirteen year old girl with severely impaired hearing, who declared that suddenly, she could hear the birds singing.

The man who had suffered from severe depression for many years with months of those years spent in psychiatric hospitals, who came to Fr Peter at the end of the week and told him that since he had been blessed and prayed with he experienced a peace he had never felt before — a peace that had lasted the entire week and which he believed would not leave him.

An elderly woman (who had travelled to Medjugorje only after a great deal of persuasion from her daughter who was concerned by the depth of grief that still burdened her following the death of her husband two years before) who also experienced a tremendous feeling of peace and acceptance after resting in the spirit when Fr Rookey blessed her.

A man with cancer, who left aside his two walking sticks, climbed the hill of Podbrdo and testified to an entire lack of pain in the days following Fr Peter's healing service.

And so many other personal stories of inner peace and seemingly physical healing that had occurred in this peaceful and spirit-filled valley, when Fr Peter Mary Rookey called on the healing power of Jesus to be poured out on the hundreds of ill and anxious people who flocked to him.

Maura Cross will never forget one such apparent healing she was witness to on a bright afternoon in Medjugorje before the outbreak of the war there. Travelling to the valley to attend the Youth 2000 festival with a group of people from London, England, she heard that Fr Peter Rookey was also in Medjugorje.

As word spread through the valley that Fr Peter would hold a healing service in one of the large green tents down behind the church, Maura made her way there with about two hundred other pilgrims.

As the service progressed, Maura's group were invited to stand in line for blessing.

"There were about fifty or sixty of us and we all stood in one long line," she recalls.

"Fr Rookey walked down the line, his hands held out over us, giving us a general blessing as he went with the crucifix held in his hand. Then he went back to the beginning of the line and began to move along it, praying over each person individually.

"Before he had even reached one woman in our group she suddenly fell back down on the ground, just as if she had been hit with something, But there was nobody or nothing near her.

"She lay there all through the healing service, as if she was asleep or dead, but when we asked Fr Peter should we rouse her he said to leave her alone."

The healing service was over, Maura recalls, and she and some other people were speaking with Fr Peter when the woman lying on the ground seemed to come round.

"She got to her feet and seemed very dazed. She came over to us, where we were gathered in a circle round Fr Peter, looked at Father and asked: 'Are you the one who did the healing? Where is the bird?'

"Needless to say we all looked at her and thought that she was imagining things, because for some minutes she seemed to be almost in another world.

"Fr Peter asked her what bird she was talking about and she replied, 'the bird that hit me'.

"I was very curious about what she said however, and as everybody left the tent I followed her and asked her would she like to have a cup of coffee with me. She agreed."

Over coffee, the other woman spoke to Maura about why she had come to Medjugorje.

It had taken Margaret Newton a couple of years before she finally made it to Medjugorje in October 1990. Every time before that when she had tried to make arrangements it was to discover that the trip was booked out.

'Don't worry' friends had told her. 'You won't go until the time is right for you, and Our Lady wants you there'. Not really understanding, she had thought it a strange thing to say.

Finally, the time had come — and in a strange way. Trying once again to book and being too late for a place, she had spent the money instead on a headstone for her mother's grave. Then had come the call — a cancellation was available. Would she take it? She was shocked. Here was the place — and now she had no money. Asking her husband what she should do he, who was not even a Catholic, told her to say yes, that the money would come from somewhere.

And it had, just in time and at long last she arrived in Medjugorje.

"I was just a bundle of pain," she says, describing her emotional state at the time.

"For years I had had so many things go wrong in my life, so much worry and anxiety and so many difficulties, that the only way I could describe myself was just one big bundle of pain, hurt and guilt. I felt so wretched and so sinful, I was under such tremendous strain and the worst thing of all was that I just could not cry."

That first morning at breakfast the others in the group were talking about healings they had heard of, and about a very special priest with a healing ministry — Fr Peter Rookey. When he laid hands on people, they said, wonderful things happened. People fell down and rested in the Spirit and many people were healed.

"I was fascinated," she recalls.

"I had never heard anything like this in my life and listened to the talk with great interest."

Later, she went to the English Mass at St James' church and afterwards Peter Cooke who had organised the pilgrimage, told the group that Fr Peter Rookey had arrived in Medjugorje and he had arranged a meeting with the group for the following day.

Margaret was amazed. Just this morning they had been talking about this healing priest and now here he was in Medjugorje — and she was going to meet him!

Next morning, the group made their way to the tent, as Maura Cross had described. When Fr Rookey arrived, Margaret was drawn immediately to him.

"It was his humility that hit me in the face," she recalls.

"He began to talk to us in the words of the Apostles Creed. Did we believe in God, the Father Almighty, maker of heaven and earth? Yes, yes, I believed in that. And he went through the creed and to everything he asked I was able to say yes.

"Then he said a strange thing. He said that God had forgiven us, but did we think we were greater than God that we could not forgive ourselves? And in my heart I suddenly knew that while God had forgiven me, I had never forgiven myself. And when Fr Rookey told us to say, I forgive myself, I said just that — I forgive me.

"Then we were asked to stand in line. We formed two lines and I was in the second. Fr Rookey walked up the first line holding his hands above the people, then he came towards my line and I thought I was going to be blessed. So I did what I always do when I am being blessed, I closed my eyes and joined my hands and bowed my head."

Her eyes closed and head bowed, Margaret was unaware that Fr Peter had passed by.

"The next thing I heard was a sudden whooshing sound, like a wind, that made me look up. And when I did I saw a small white bird, a dove, in a white light with sheets of red flame coming from it, and it hit me on the side of the forehead and I remember falling backwards onto the ground."

Lying on the ground, Margaret was partly aware of what was going on around her. When she tried to move however, she found she couldn't lift either her head, her arms or her legs.

"And then, as if they were being squeezed out of me, tears suddenly began to flow out of my eyes, oceans and oceans of tears, like I had never cried before."

When she eventually managed to sit up she recalls saying something about the bird that hit her. They had brought her to Fr Rookey then and she told him what she had seen.

"He smiled at me and he just kept saying, 'Thank you Jesus. Praise you Jesus'.

Afterwards, Margaret says, she felt so different, full of an extraordinary joy and peace and love. It was some time later — and after her return home — that she realised she had indeed received a tremendous healing from all the pain she had carried with her for so long. And the healing has remained with her right to this day.

Before she had felt so full of pain, so wretched and sinful, now she feels a tremendous peace and joy. And so many of the difficulties in her life have been healed and changed, so that the peace has spilled out onto everything around her.

Her experience was an extraordinary one, she admits, but is true in every detail.

"I'm just an ordinary housewife with a husband and children. I could never have made up a story like that," she says with deep simplicity.

But it's an experience that has changed her life — and one that she shares with anybody who asks.

"Now," she says, "when people talk about their being no God, I tell them how wrong they are. There is a God, and a Jesus, and a Holy Spirit. I know there's a Holy Spirit — because I saw Him."

Chapter Seventeen

BEGGING FOR HEALING

What would you say to a person who has been healed, I ask Fr Peter?

"To stay close to God, who has done this wonderful thing for them," he replies.

"If they want to have a continuation of that healing they should remain close to Jesus.

"I know what I said to the young man in Balham, London a couple of years ago. He was suffering from AIDS and I asked him whether he wanted to be healed of this. He said yes, he did want healing, so I told him that he must give up this lifestyle he had followed and give himself to the Lord instead. And he did that and I prayed with him and he experienced the love of Jesus in his life."

The dramatic healing which was claimed made the front page of at least one newspaper at the time. The young man, who gave his full name to the people who had organised the healing service, was persuaded by friends to keep his identity secret to protect his family, but later said that he was willing to sign a statement testifying to his healing and to give his doctor permission to confirm it.

"Our Lord Himself said to the man at the pool in Bethsaida, after He had healed him, to go and sin no more, as He so often said to people," Fr Rookey adds.

Does that mean if a person is healed, then returns to their old lifestyle, God will take back the healing, I ask?

"Well, that would be up to the Lord," smiles Fr Peter, "but the greater disaster than losing their healing would be losing their soul. Then the healing would have been in vain."

So often, I recall, when healing people Jesus told them their sins were forgiven. Does this mean that confession is an important consideration in the healing ministry?

"The Sacrament of Reconciliation is indeed a very beautiful expression of God's love and healing power," says Fr Peter.

"It's a very refreshing Sacrament, washing us clean, giving a great lift to our lives. It's a meeting with Jesus and if we enter into it with faith seeing the confessor, no matter who he is, as God speaking to us, God being made present to us, then it's a very strengthening thing in our lives.

"It's also part of God's healing work in us. As is the Miracle Prayer, which is an invitation to leave our former way of life and give ourselves entirely to the Lord, give our great 'YES' to Him."

'Dear Fr Rookey,

There are no words to express our heartfelt gratitude to you for your most compassionate kindness. Your blessed visit to my son, who is severely afflicted with multiple sclerosis, was truly a 'Heart's Gift' (from the Heart of Christ).

I want you to know that although he was not physically healed, your visiting him seemed to bring a peace which has remained with him and renewed his spirit for at least some improvement in his condition.

His sufferings are so great in many ways, but he bears them with great courage. I am very proud of him. Only Our

Mother of Sorrows understands how I feel to see my only son like this.

May God continue to bless all your fine endeavours in the healing ministry. May Our Blessed Mother always keep you safe under her loving care.' (California)

Susan looked round the church just before the healing Mass started and wondered where so many people had come from. Everywhere she looked, the church appeared packed to capacity and beyond, every seat full and crowds standing three and four deep along the walls, up the aisles and right onto the altar steps.

In all her life, she thought, she had never seen so many ill people.The ones who affected her most were the children — so many seriously ill-looking children, that suddenly she felt guilty even being there. How dare she sit here hoping for healing while these sick, weak children needed a miracle even more than she did.

But she was desperate enough to come here in hope, she realised, her own two small children strongly in her mind. If only she could have a second chance at life to be with them as they grew up, to be able to do all the things other mothers could.

She had been devastated when the neurologist had given his diagnosis. Multiple sclerosis — it hadn't seemed possible, not for somebody like herself, an ambitious and successful company director in her thirties, with everything in the world to look forward to.

Couldn't there be a mistake, she remembered asking. The specialist had shaken his head. She had all the symptoms, he pointed out. It had begun with a terrible tiredness, she recalled now. An abnormal sort of tiredness that she just couldn't shake off no matter how she tried. At first she had put it down to the pressures of combining a demanding career with being a wife and mother. The doctor had thought so too, decided she was suffering from lack of Vitamin B12 and put her on a course of tablets.

They hadn't helped at all, she remembered. Then, over a number of months she began to experience other symptoms — tingling in her fingers and her feet, pain in her eyes, blurred vision, pains in the spine, muscle spasms, the loss of power in her leg.

She'd spent eight days in hospital undergoing a series of tests including the MRI, one of the most sophisticated scans in the world for detecting abnormalities and diseases of the central nervous system. The MRI had shown up a number of things, she was told, including spots on the spinal chord. Their diagnosis could unfortunately only be one of MS. A lumbar puncture would be done, but would only confirm the diagnosis and give a fuller picture of her condition. They were really very sorry they could offer her no other diagnosis.

Both she and her husband had been devastated.

"We just didn't know how to cope with the diagnosis at first," she recalls.

"We both cried. I have never felt so broken in all my life, but over the next while we tried to come to terms with it. We talked about the future and how the illness would progress and what we would do at each stage, how we would cope. I joined the MS society and read every piece of literature I could about the illness. The future looked frightening."

One day her mother-in-law gave her a little card with something called the Miracle Prayer printed on it.

"I suppose you could say that I had lost my faith," Susan says today.

"It was years since I had been to Mass, but when she gave me the card and told me about the priest she'd read about, who performed healing Masses, I was so desperate that I was ready to try anything."

She began praying the Miracle Prayer, she says, storming heaven three and four times a day, begging the God she had forgotten about for so many years to come to her aid now in this moment of terrible trouble.

A couple of days before the healing Mass she had a lumbar puncture. It would be about three weeks, they told her, before they would have results.

Then had come the afternoon of the Mass in the beautiful and large church of the Passionist Fathers, Mount Argus, Dublin.

As the priests came out onto the altar, Susan searched among them for the 'healing priest' she had heard so much about. When he began to speak, praying with them before the Mass then explaining what format it would take, she was surprised by the strange mixture of humour and spirituality. He was undoubtedly, she felt, one of the most human priests she had ever encountered. And the Mass, when it began, surprised her too.

"If I had been amazed at the number of people there," she recalls, "I was even more surprised by the intense spirituality of the congregation. I found the whole thing intensely emotional, inspiring and overwhelming. There was so much devotion — such an air of spirituality that even I, who had found Mass so uninspiring that I had stopped going, was immensely touched.

"After Communion, Fr Rookey came down among the congregation with the monstrance containing the Host, to bless the people and to pray for our healing.

"I was at the edge of a seat, quite near the front, and he stopped right in front of me, holding the Host up above me. I remember looking at the Host and begging for healing, and suddenly I began to cry. I just sat there and I cried and cried and no matter how I tried to stop, the tears kept coming. I couldn't understand it myself. I remember feeling mortified in front of so many people, but the tears kept coming. Then, just three rows in front of me, a young girl with cerebral palsy suddenly got out of her seat, handed her crutches to her mother and walked across the church and up onto the altar. I have never seen anything like it in my life."

Susan left the church later that afternoon feeling, she says, as if something special had touched her life.

"I knew I had been touched in some way, if only that my faith had been restored to me. Once I managed to stop crying I felt utterly peaceful and relaxed, a feeling that stayed with me for days.

"A week later I visited my doctor, as routine, and after examining me he said in great surprise that the power had come back into my leg. I said I knew this, and told him that besides this I had no pain either. He was completely taken aback."

A few weeks later she visited her specialist, one of Ireland's leading neurologists, to receive the results of the lumbar puncture.

"He didn't know quite what to say to me," Susan remembers vividly.

"Despite my experience during the Mass and the return of the power to my leg and the absence of the pain, my husband

and I went into this consultation as well prepared as we could be for the bad results we knew must be coming.

"The specialist looked at us and eventually said that he was sorry, that he was unable to confirm the diagnosis of MS, because it hadn't shown up in the lumbar puncture. The fluid test was completely clear. He just couldn't understand it, he continued. All the symptoms, all the indications following the MRI had proven to their satisfaction that their original diagnosis was correct. Yet now, the fluid just didn't confirm this. All he could say, he finally told us, was that I did not have MS.

"We just couldn't believe it, but we eventually left feeling dazed. I can tell you however, that when the reality hit us, the entire family celebrated that night."

And that was it, she says. Almost six months later she is well, happy and full of energy.

"I can only say that I have been at the peak of my health ever since, not just well but really well and so full of energy that I am amazed myself.

"Before the Mass I had been feeling so bad, so ill, that all I wanted to do was leave work, stay at home and make my life easier because I just couldn't cope with the illness.

"Now I have, literally, a new lease of life, the business has expanded and my life is going from strength to strength.

"Now and again I stop and wonder at it all, and wonder is it all really true, have I been really cured? But I can't disagree with the medical evidence. It's just so difficult to take in — that just last November I was facing an uncertain and pain-filled future, and now everything is so different.

"And I believe and know that if I hadn't gone to that healing Mass, the diagnosis of MS would not have changed. Something wonderful and special happened to me that day."

Chapter Eighteen

A NEW TOMORROW

'Dear Fr Rookey,

Praise God! I was healed!

I had severe anxiety for nine months. It was so bad I couldn't work. I felt like I was going to have a heart attack twenty-four hours a day. I had most of the symptoms. From August 1992 thru May 1993 I had taken 407 doses of medication. The medication wasn't working and I was told I might require anxiety medication the rest of my life. It was obvious to me I needed a miracle from God.

On May 28th 1993 I came in faith to your Healing Mass. When you touched my head and prayed that I be 'free from anxiety', I felt a calm come over me and it hasn't left. Praise God!

One June 25th I met with Father and told him of my healing and thanked him for having you at his church. Although I have been coming to your healing service for the last two and a half years, this was the first time I requested healing for myself. The other fourteen times I requested healing for a member of my family.

The reason I promote your healing ministry is very simple. You are performing your service in the same way Jesus did two thousand years ago. Jesus taught and healed. You have the gift of healing from the Holy Spirit per 1 Cor. 12. You are truly a Man of God! You are doing it God's way. May God pour out his blessings on you for your beautiful ministry and for doing it His way! The Church needs more Fr Rookeys!

Sincerely in God's love.' (Arizona)

It's almost midnight as Fr Peter steps out into the quiet darkness of Reggie Donnelly's garden in west Belfast. His arm round the shoulders of the former baker and trade unionist whom he calls his 'right arm' when he visits Northern Ireland, he holds back his head to look up at the clear star-filled sky above him.

Here in the province where his ministry began and which for the last twenty-five years has experienced the agony of division and hatred, he feels strangely at peace. Holding up his arms to the God he loves and serves, he murmurs a prayer for peace, reconciliation and healing for this deeply divided community.

The night has been full of memories, so many people coming up to him after the Mass to remind him of visits he had made here before, of healings that occurred and conversions that had happened.

It was the end of yet another two-week visit to the land of his forebears. He remembered the first time he had arrived in Ireland, way back in 1948. It was August, late summer in this island, but the whole country had been as green as if the Almighty Himself had painted it so. One field richer and deeper than another, divided by hedges just as green, dotted by tall and ancient trees and grey stone houses.

It was here that he had first been made aware that God had mapped out a special ministry for him.

Perhaps he should have realised it beforehand, he mused now, but the signs that God had given him of what was to come had not registered on his mind.

The very first had been in connection with his own mother, whose faith and devotion had surely led to the return of his sight and had set him on the path to the priesthood.

He remembered now, the various times when away in the priesthood his family had called him for his help and prayers.

Johanna Rookey had developed cancer, the illness wasting her body and painting lines of pain on her beautiful face. She had all but died, on several occasions, her hold on this life less strong than her closeness to the next. They had called him then, telephoning him wherever he was to come home and to pray with her. And he had done so, anointing her with the holy oil and blessing her with the crucifix containing the relics of the saints. And though she would have more than one foot in the grave, she would come back to life.

So there had been something there even then, he knew, though at the time he had put it all down to the anointing and to the Servite saints.

"Tired, Father?" Reggie asks anxiously. It has been a long day, a busy two weeks that would have taxed the strength of a man half his age.

Fr Peter shakes his head.

"Would you admit it, Father?" the Belfast man asks and Fr Peter laughs.

"Time enough to rest when I'm dead," he says.

"But if the Lord permits it, I'll go on serving Him for some time to come."

Some six miles away at her farmhouse home in north Belfast, just a few miles outside the city, Geraldine McIlwaine tucked the bedcovers round her sleeping son before stooping to kiss him on the forehead. She wished that Kevin, her husband, could see him now, he was getting so big and looking so well these days. But Kevin, who had been with her through the years of Ryan's illness, was with God now, taken from them following a massive coronary last year.

Looking at the face of her sleeping son, Geraldine's mind goes back over the years of pain and worry before the amazing experience with the healing priest from Chicago.

She'd never heard of him before going to the healing service that night in Holy Cross Chapel, with her aunt and her mother. It was her aunt who had told her about Fr Rookey, that when he laid hands on people they were healed. The service was that night. Geraldine hadn't been sure if she'd make it, but just about managed to get there before the service began.

She would have tried anything, she knew, to have her son made well.

Ryan was only two and a half years old when they realised that something was wrong. He wasn't well and no matter how she tried to feed him, he just couldn't seem to put on weight. The doctor sent them to the hospital where they carried out tests, but could find nothing wrong. Perhaps his body was simply rejecting fat, they said, and for the next three years Geraldine brought him to the hospital clinic every six months.

Then, in 1989, they carried out a brain scan. It showed up a massive tumour behind the little boy's right eye. It was a very rare type of tumour, Geraldine and Kevin were told, and very little was known about its type in the western world.

"It was a nightmare," Geraldine recalls.

"After attending the clinic for so long we had been sure that nothing serious was wrong, or surely they would have discovered it by now. But here we were, faced with this dreadful news. They told us then that it was probably there from birth, or soon after."

They had taken him into hospital then and operated on the tumour, removing as much as they could. Ryan was in that hospital for three days before being referred to Beaver Park, the cancer hospital. Every day for six weeks the little boy underwent treatment, Geraldine and Kevin spending every available moment with him.

It was during this time that Geraldine's aunt had heard about the healing service.

They had been brought to the front of the church with other seriously ill people. When the service was due to start, five priests came out onto the altar.

"I didn't know which one was Fr Rookey," says Geraldine. "I'd never seen or heard of him before, but when the priests came out I picked him out immediately. There was just something very different about him.

"He spoke to us first, telling us about the healing ministry and about some of the people who had been healed by God. Then he invited us all to go up, in lines, for the anointing with oil, and blessing."

As each line stood at the altar steps, Fr Rookey passed down it once holding his hands in the air, blessing the people as he moved but not placing his hands on any individual. Then he walked back up to the top of the line again, to start blessing each person individually. When the line in front of her had been blessed, Geraldine moved forward carrying Ryan in her arms. Fr Rookey passed down the line, then as he moved back up again towards the top, stopped suddenly in front of Geraldine. Reggie Donnelly, who was beside him and was holding the oil for the anointing, tried to urge him forward to the top of the line, but the priest stayed where he was.

'Who is ill,' he asked Geraldine.

'My little boy, Father,' she replied.

'What is wrong with him?' Fr Peter asked.

'He has a brain tumour, Father,' Geraldine replied.

"I can remember getting this incredible feeling going through me," Geraldine says, "and I began to cry. No matter how hard I tried, I couldn't stop the tears pouring out of my eyes and down onto Ryan's anorak. Fr Rookey had been looking at the child, but then he looked up and saw my face and I'll never forget his words. 'The beautiful tears of a mother,' he said. Then he blessed Ryan with the holy oil and with the crucifix and blessed me too. And I felt something very special, even though another part of my mind was wondering why he had suddenly stopped in front of us — and why could I not stop crying."

The priest's sudden stop in front of the ill child had a tremendous effect on the rest of the congregation. For a week or two afterwards, everywhere she went Geraldine was stopped by people enquiring was she the mother of the little boy that Fr Rookey had stopped to bless.

Ryan was brought back to continue his treatment, she recalls, then another routine scan was done to see whether the treatment was having any effect at all.

"The results were amazing," says Geraldine.

"The doctors were over the moon about it — they'd never seen such results before, they said. The tumour had shrunk to the size of a pinhead and looked set to shrink even further, they felt."

Over the next three months Ryan attended the local hospital. They were amazed by his progress. No sickness or other symptoms, and then he began to put on weight very rapidly until soon, Geraldine says, he was a fine strong looking child.

"Absolutely brilliant — amazing," said an Australian doctor who was attached to the hospital, as time passed by and the chances of the tumour reoccurring grew fainter and fainter. And before long they were able to take him off specific medication that they had said he would need until he was at least fourteen years old, due to the fact that the tumour had irritated the pituitary gland.

The medical people might marvel at the extraordinary effectiveness of the radiotherapy, Geraldine thought, as she turned out the bedside lamp beside Ryan.

But in her heart, she believed it was much more, that the blessing Ryan had received that night from Fr Rookey had achieved the amazing healing.

Closing the bedroom door and going back down to the kitchen, she felt Kevin's loss keenly. They had been through the nightmare together, had attended the clinics, worried and prayed that things would work out differently to the doctors' fears. And they had. And Kevin had been there to see Ryan's life suddenly come together again.

Feeling the tears prickling at her eyelids, Geraldine did what she always did when she felt lonely and down. Going to the little card sellotaped to the kitchen wall she began to say Fr Rookey's Miracle Prayer.

And a peace, deep and gentle and full of love crept through her mind, wiping away the tears and promising her all the strength she needed to face a new tomorrow...

It's over twelve years since I wrote the book you have just read, about one of the most inspiring people I have ever met during a journalistic career that has spanned over thirty years.
It is not a statement that I make lightly.

During those years, as journalist and author, I have met and interviewed some of the most interesting people of these times. The list runs from politicians and presidents, to leading names in the worlds of music and movies. It includes a multitude of "ordinary" people who have achieved quite extraordinary achievements, and others who have experienced the very depths of inhumanity from their fellow human beings.

Most especially, however, it includes three saintly people who have each, in their own unique way, demonstrated so forcibly to me the extent of God's love and power and compassion in this world He has created.

The first of these is Pope Paul VIth, whom I had the great privilege of meeting within the Vatican in Holy Year 1975, and from where, as a journalist, I carried back his personal message to the women of Ireland.

Still a member of the Protestant Church of Ireland faith at the time (which I had been born into, but from which I have since converted to the Roman Catholic faith), I was deeply touched by his saintly gentleness and the deep warm kindness which shone from his eyes – so different to the photographs and pictures which had seemed to show an austere, even cold personality. Among my most treasured possessions are the photographs taken at the time, which throughout our meeting show him gently holding my hands in his, only releasing them to give me his blessing.

The second of these latter-day saints is Blessed Mother Theresa of Calcutta, whom I was greatly privileged to meet and talk with during her last ever visit to Ireland. All other interviews had been cancelled due to the fall which had fractured her ribs, but through the efforts of a priest friend who worked with her Little Sisters of the Poor, I achieved the seemingly impossible. Very early one morning, I joined Mother Theresa and her Sisters and two priests for their morning prayers, kneeling directly behind Mother on a cold hard floor for so long that I couldn't help moving often while she, despite her pain, never stirred an inch.

Later, I travelled with her throughout the day while she attended Mass, met numerous people, and spoke movingly to priests and seminarians in the beautiful and ancient chapel in the Catholic university of Maynooth. And after we spoke, about her life and her work and the God she loved, she took my hands in both of hers and challenged me never to be afraid to do God's will in my life.

And now I come to the third of these very special people, so powerfully touched by the love of God and so deeply motivated to fearlessly following Him in their lives.

I was working for the Irish national broadcasting station, Radio Telefis Eireann, when the telephone rang on my desk and a voice on the other end invited me to come over to the studios and meet "this extraordinary healing priest, Fr. Peter Rookey, who's been credited with miraculous healings".

My initial response was that miracles didn't happen these days, and it was with some considerable skepticism that I walked across to the television studios on the other side of the complex.

The black-robed priest who was just about to go on a live afternoon programme was something of a surprise. No fire, thunder and brimstone – but a wonderful sense of humour and a warmth that had infected the entire TV crew. And when, at the end of the live interview, he held out his arms and prayed a healing blessing on the watching viewers around the country, all those in the studio experienced something deeply touching and very unusual. Within minutes of the end of the broadcast, while the station's telephone lines went into what one senior administrator described as "melt-down", I was amazed to see almost every staff member – producers, presenters, camera crew and backroom staff – line up for personal blessings. And when Fr. Rookey placed his hands on their heads and invoked the healing power of the Holy Spirit and the Saints, several fell back in what appeared to be a trance, and were laid out on the hard studio floor where they remained "asleep" for some minutes.

That was the beginning of my great friendship and deep admiration for this wonderful man of God, this "A Man of Miracles" as he is so aptly named in the title of this book. And over the years since I have been privileged to meet with Fr. Peter in many places and in different countries, and to witness the tremendous gift of God's healing power through his laying on of hands.

It's a work that this Servite priest has continued over the years since I first researched the book you have just read, and still does to this day through the Chicago based International Compassion Ministry.

Many of those healed have never even met Fr. Peter Rookey. But they have heard of him, and have telephoned the Ministry desperately seeking his prayers, and have come back talking of answers to those prayers.

Of healings, in mind, body or spirit. Of perhaps the first real experience of the love of God in their lives. And of times when although physical healing has not been granted, they have felt peace and acceptance and the very real knowledge of God's tremendous love and care, especially for the most broken hearted.

Today, a wonderfully young 88 years old and over sixty-three years an ordained priest, Fr. Peter's service and dedication to the healing ministry that God has chosen for him is as powerful as ever.

His mailbox continues daily to bear testimony to this ministry and its results, from all over the United States and beyond; from

Australia to the Philippines; from every part of Europe to the South Americas, and almost every point between. Countless stories of healings from physical illnesses and psychological and psychiatric disorders - even to those of release from the possession of evil.

"Anna" is one of these. A young woman in her mid-twenties from Eastern Europe, she had suffered all her life from the results of being unloved, unwanted and from cruel violence, much from within her home and family. On hearing that Fr. Peter Rookey was to visit her native city in late 2004, she wrote him this heartfelt plea, translated from her own language.

"Dear Father Peter Rookey,
I salute you, Father, from the depth of my heart.
In my life, I have experienced a lot of cruel violence (including home/family violence) that has led to many traumas, anxieties and phobias. I have been under exorcists' care for several years.
I am asking you, Father, for your immediate prayer for all my intentions. I have listed an attachment to this letter. I especially ask the Lord for a grace of my soul's full deliverance from demonic possessions, all post-traumatic symptoms, anxieties and phobias. It is my desire to come to Lowicz and to attend the prayers there. I ask you for your sacerdotal blessings."

Fr. Peter recalls, with great joy, the deliverance of six young possessed people during that overseas trip. Anna was one of these. "She had four demons of hatred within her" he recalls.
"One was Satan."

She grew up feeling unloved and unwanted. Already, five officially designated exorcist priests from various dioceses had prayed over her to attempt to deliver her from these hate-demons.

The need to be released, as expressed in her poignant letter, led Anna to visit three times the churches in which Fr. Peter was saying Mass and praying for the healing of those present.

These demons tortured her while, with priests and with the

faithful continuously praying, we sought to release her," Fr. Peter recalls.

"We prayed over her with the Blessed Sacrament, anointed her and used much Blessed Water. It took six strong men to hold her down, and she spat on us repeatedly, while cursing us. After long sessions of intense prayer, the demons left her."

Later, both Anna and the priest who was her spiritual director wrote an account of the experience. And one evening, Anna stood up in the church and told a hushed congregation how it was the intense love with which Fr. Peter and his fellow priests surrounded her that finally cast out the torturing demons of hatred.

The following is from that testimony.

"I can now invoke God's help using both Jesus and Mary's names, which I was unable to invoke before that.

"I could, without fear, go to confession, kneel at the confessional and confess in the Divine Mercy Sanctuary. For many years, even looking at confessionals has made me fearful and filled with abomination. I was unable to overcome those feelings whenever I stood close to a confessional.

"I can receive Holy Communion with joy, without internal fear and resistance which I had before.

"For the first time, after receiving Holy Communion without fear, I have been overjoyed and peaceful to an indescribable extent.

"I can pray normally, without fear and without avoidance of some phrases that I was unable or did not want to speak out before. I feel calm and free, with no trace of paralyzing feelings that usually affected me and stopped me from praying.

"I have been an unwanted and unloved child from the beginning. I have constantly experienced cruelty and violence, rejection and humiliation from my family members. They had always treated me like the worst and unworthy person. I have not experienced a caring love from them. Nobody cared about my human needs.

I lived in constant fear, without any hope that anybody would love me. Rather, I was convinced that I would always be rejected because I was unworthy to be accepted and loved.

"I feared people. I feared God. I thought that God rejected me too and that He did not love me either. Since a few priests afflicted me, I began to fear priests even more.

"Fr. Peter, within a few minutes during my meeting with him, showed me more concern and love than I had ever experienced in my life. He embraced me like the best father. He did not reject me. He showed me his compassion. It has made me believe that Lord Jesus does not reject me, that He loves me – that the more I am rejected by others, the more I am loved by Him!

"Jesus has taken away my fears that I had of Him and of His priests.

"Fr. Peter, through his prayers and his love to people, which I could see in him, helped me to overcome the temptation arising in me, that day, to leave the church and instead to stop to pray.

"Glory be to Jesus!"

Anna's story is just one of so many that continue to pour into the office of the International Compassion Ministry. As the volunteer staff take numerous telephone messages for heartfelt pleas for prayer – so many that often even the night-time answering machine runs out of memory – the 88 year old Servant of Mary at its heart never ceases to praise God for His love for mankind, and for the loving intercession of His Mother in the lives of so many.

Every day, the results of that love are shown in the Ministry's postbag.

"Dear Fr. Rookey,
In January you prayed with me that the tumour found in my pancreas would not be cancer.

I had an MRI yesterday to identify the tumour and to look for possible liver tumours also. My doctor called me today and said "there is nothing in the pancreas or the liver. There is no tumour. The tumour is no longer there. Praised be Jesus Christ. Thank you, Fr. Rookey, for praying with me and for sending me the healing cloths. I will work harder now for my God and Church in thanksgiving for this miracle." (Mont Clare)

"Dear Fr. Rookey,
I am writing to you to praise and thank God for the gift of healing I received after you blessed me over the phone on the feast of St. Teresa of Avila.
I had ten operations over a number of years on my abdomen...... I was told that they did not know whether, after the next operation, I would have enough bowel left to live......I was unable to go to daily Mass. My parish priest had anointed me the previous week.

After you blessed me, I didn't feel anything different at first, but I felt hopeful. I told my husband: 'That was the strangest blessing I've ever had, but I think I've been healed'. When you told me 'Be healed' it was like a command. You sounded so sure.........At 5 a.m. I woke up and was able to move my bowels normally without pain. That morning I was able to get dressed and go to Mass myself........My bowel is working normally for the first time in years. I have not had to take medication since that night.....I am praying for you. I thank God every day many times over for the new life I am living. May God bless and keep you always." (Ireland)

"Dearest Fr. Peter,
Fifty years ago, on the Feast of the Assumption of the Blessed Virgin Mary, you came to our house to pray over me. I was four years old and quite ill with rheumatic fever....Because I was ill my crib was placed in the living room opposite the beautiful marble fireplace..... You arrived early in the morning, greeted my father before he left for work and told my mother you would need nothing. She excused herself to the kitchen and you placed a white alb around your neck, kissing it in reverence as you did so. Upon the mantle you placed two lit candles and a crucifix to become your altar. Some of the time you prayed quietly and sometimes you said things out loud, but in a foreign language to me. However, what stood out in my young mind was that you knelt on the marble hearth without a pillow for many, many hours.....You came to my bedside and touched my head once and smiled so tenderly, not wanting to scare me with all the Latin stuff. My mother offered you water and food but you politely refused. You left as quietly as you came......However, it now dawns on me after fifty years that perhaps I never thanked you. You prayed to the Blessed Virgin Mary and her Son that my life would be spent here on earth longer than was thought possible. You were one of the very first "shepherds" that came into my life and I now want the privilege of thanking you for all those hours of intense prayer and compassion, some fifty years ago." (Wisconsin)

"Dear Fr. Rookey,
My green-grocer gave me the name of a lady who had not left her house for six months. She was a manic depressive. I phoned you for prayers for her.

Yesterday, he informed me that she had taken herself on a holiday, interstate, to visit her sister. Her family and her doctor were amazed. Praise God! We send our love and prayers to you. God bless you always." (Australia)

"Dear Fr. Rookey,
When our grandson was to have a bone marrow transplant we told you he was in intensive care, fighting for life as he caught pneumonia. Your touch of mercy was a gift from heaven, and a presence in his room led to a wonderful miracle. He was miraculously healed! The doctors and nurses were left speechless as he began to recover.

Our grandson is all boy now. He is a handful. Praise to Jesus Christ, our living Saviour!! The power of prayer has taught us never to give up and that is why we love you." (Texas)

"Dear Fr. Rookey,
A few weeks ago I phoned for a blessing in hopes of a healing of my cancer which had been diagnosed in 4th stage at four different places. You prayed with me and recommended St. Peregrine as intercessor.

I learned from the specialist that there is no sign of tumour in my chest and the lungs are clear except for a smudge on the lining. My appetite has returned and I've gained the weight back that I had lost. My blood count is down considerably. ..Thank you so very much." (California)

Dear Fr. Rookey,
On January 19th our doctor called us and told us my husband had prostate cancer. We asked for your prayer that it hadn't spread. After you prayed, he felt the pain for about a minute, and then it left.

The bone scan came out clear! He went ahead and had his prostate removed and the doctor was pleasantly surprised. All tests for spreading to lymph nodes were negative! Praise the Lord, and you, Father." (Minnesota)

In his monthly newsletter in November 2004, Fr. Peter Rookey thanked all of those associates of the International Compassion Ministry for their prayerful support. In the previous two months, he observed, counting telephone calls, letters, faxes, personal contacts and websites, approximately 10,000 persons were touched spiritually and physically by the Ministry. So many of these had asked for healing for families. And Fr. Peter quoted Pope John Paul II when he had said that the family's greatest weapons were the Eucharist and the Rosary.

Over the years I have known Fr. Peter Rookey, I have many wonderful memories of times spent with him.

Of walking through the vineyards and along the dusty roads in Medjugorje, Bosnia-Hercegovina (where the Mother of God is reported to have been appearing daily since June 24th 1981), following the sandal-prints in the red earth of this black-robed priest who stopped so patiently, and so often, to bless pilgrims from many nations.

Of standing for hours among a crowd of almost 10,000 people who had been unable to get into a small packed church on a hillside on the west coast of Ireland, and who waited and prayed in the cold night air until their turn came to receive a blessing.

Of weeping in a church several hours journey away from Chicago, as a woman cried tears of joy while she pushed her empty wheelchair back down the centre aisle followed by her elated family.

Of laughing while the congregation of a busy European city centre church almost lifted the ancient roof from the building as they joined Fr. Peter in one of his favourite songs of praise, 'The Battle Hymn of the Republic'.

Of feeling, so strongly, such a much-loved member of the great and mystical body of the Church as this humble priest of God, Servant of Mary, held up the Body of Christ in a poverty-stricken ghetto area, and the rays of the setting sun reflected a myriad of beautiful colours through the bullet-damaged panes of the chapel's stained glass windows.

Throughout the centuries, and particularly at times when mankind so greatly needs it, God has sent His special messengers to witness to His eternal love and mercy.
I have no doubt that Fr. Peter Rookey, O.S .M. is one of these.

Heather Parsons (March 2005)

Fr. Rookey may be contacted at the following address:

International Compassion Ministry,
Fr. Peter M. Rookey, O.S.M.
20180 Governors Highway,
Room 203,
Olympia Fields, IL 60461-1067

Tel.(708)748-6279
Fax. (708)748-0234
www.smcenter.org\frrookey.htm